Seventy-five Years

of the

Minneapolis Aquatennial

Seventy-five Years
of the
Minneapolis Aquatennial

Pam Albinson

foreword by Barbara Flanagan

NODIN PRESS

Design and layout: John Toren
Archival research and support: Jack Kabrud, Curator, Hennepin History Museum; Susan Larson-Fleming, Archivist, Hennepin History Museum

Photo credits:
All photos are from the collection of the Hennepin County Museum with the following exceptions:
page 53 – Rachel Kytonen/Isanti County News
page 130 – Life Time—The Healthy Way of Life Company
page 124, 125, 129, 136-9, 140, 153, 155, 165 – Minneapolis Downtown Council
page 132 – Susan Lesch
page 140 – Richard Wesley Wong
front cover, lower right: Matt Olson Photography
front cover, middle left: Joe Michaud-Scorza

ISBN: 978-1-935666-66-0

Library of Congress Control Number: 2014938436

Published by
Nodin Press, LLC
5114 Cedar Lake Road
Minneapolis, MN 55416

Printed in U.S.A.

To Norton Stillman, Owner, Publisher of Nodin Press, whose life-long love of Aquatennial and generosity of spirit made this book possible;

To the Aquatennial visionaries and thousands of volunteers, the unsung heroes, who have brought the "visions of the visionaries" to life;

To the participants and spectators who make it all worthwhile.

And, to the memory of Kenneth R. Walstad, esteemed Executive Vice President/Managing Director of the Minneapolis Aquatennial. His guiding philosophy encompassed the belief that "a festival's worth is measured not only in the contribution to the community, but also in the challenge and satisfaction it provides to its life breath – the individual volunteer." He is a legend held in the highest regard by the Aquatennial family of friends.

May this book "open the floodgates of memories and cast a nostalgic glow that will warm you for years to come."

"YOU'RE GONNA' LOVE IT!"

a favorite Walstad phrase

First Annual Minneapolis
AQUATENNIAL 1940

CONTENTS

FOREWORD

The people who handle the "once upon a timeliness" factor in our great world have hit it big.

The Minneapolis Aquatennial is seventy-five.

Once upon a time, if I may, in 1940 some bright Minneapolis businessmen got together and created a summer festival. It was based on our city lakes, our more than 10,000 lakes in Minnesota, and the mighty Mississippi River.

What's more, another bright guy named it the Minneapolis Aquatennial. It has thrived ever since, and we are glad.

The Aquatennial is aimed at everyone, whether you are sporty or not. One of the early events was the Paul Bunyan Canoe Derby that ran 450 miles down the Mississippi from Bemidji, Minnesota, to Minneapolis. The events also included the Aqua Follies, which featured well-known swimmers and divers in a week-long series of afternoon and evening entertainments at Wirth Lake. And then there were always the parades, the splendid, gloriously spectacular parades.

One of the major events was the coronation of the Queen of the Lakes. She was selected from among a group of Minnesota girls, all nice, pleasant girls who had won contests in their hometowns and were awarded a trip to the big city.

From 1948 until 1962, I covered the Aquatennial for the then morning newspaper, the *Minneapolis Tribune*. In 1952 I went to Europe with one of the queens and continued to accompany them off and on for the next ten years.

The queens were talented and often did things you didn't suspect. One, for example, ended up modeling wonderful clothes by Gabrielle Chanel of Paris. She did it so well that Madame Chanel stopped by and almost smiled at her. Another girl tried bull fighting. It was okay, nothing spectacular. And the 1962 Queen of the Lakes, Pam Albinson, has written this book.

When you read it, enjoy your memories. Or, if you are seeing the Aquatennial for the first time, put some memories together for next year, or the year after.

And remember, it's only twenty-five years until we celebrate 100 years for the Aquatennial. That's not too long to wait. And it is something to wait for.

Once upon a time . . .

~ Barbara Flanagan

W. R. STEPHENS
GENERAL CHAIRMAN

LYLE WRIGHT
BUSINESS MANAGER
AT 6401

June 26, 1940

AQUATENNIAL GENERAL
EXECUTIVE COMMITTEE

HENRY BAKER
SAM GALE
TOM HASTINGS
NEIL MESSICK
E. T. PALMER
WALTER P. QUIST
W. R. STEPHENS

Dear Mr. Stephens:

Three months ago the name "Minneapolis Aquatennial" meant nothing.
Now, it is rapidly gaining tremendous recognition. Few of us
realize what an outstanding annual national event it is going to
be. However, we cannot expect outsiders to appreciate it unless
we describe it to them completely and graphically.

With that in mind, an elaborate and beautiful souvenir program will
be issued. It will be off the press Monday, July 1, 1940. It will
be 32 pages in full color with beautiful full color photographs of
Minneapolis and our 10,000 lakes country. It will describe the
Aquatennial and give a full program of every event. IT WILL CARRY
NO ADVERTISING. It will sell for only 10 cents and will be the
only printed program for sale.

For those desiring personally or through their business to give a
preview of the Aquatennial to out-of-town friends and business con-
tacts, we announce an advance sale of these programs at 10 cents,
INCLUDING MAILING ENVELOPE. The time is short. If you desire a
quantity of the programs, please fill in the attached card and
mail it immediately so that a supply will reach you promptly the
first of next week.

The FIRST Aquatennial will be the hardest to promote. This program has been designed to promote not only the Aquatennial but
Minneapolis and its place in the whole northwestern vacationland.
If you are contemplating any mailing to anyone, this program will
be ideal. It will be the most elaborate and beautiful souvenir
program for a civic event that has ever been published and widely
distributed. PLEASE ORDER YOUR REQUIREMENTS TODAY!

Enthusiastically yours,

W. R. Stephens, General Chairman

The Minneapolis Aquatennial festival was conceived by a group of prominent Minneapolis businessmen on a business trip together to Winnipeg, Canada. During their visit, they observed a well-attended parade honoring King George VI and Queen Elizabeth, and it occurred to them that their own city ought to sponsor a festival of some kind. No doubt the success of the Winter Carnival, which had been revived two years earlier with great success across the river in Saint Paul, also played a part in their inspiration. The business contingent consisted of W.R. "Win" Stephens, the owner of Stephens

Buick; Neil Messick, manager of the Nicollet Hotel;, D.W. "Dave" Onan, whose firm, D.W. Onan and Sons, Inc., manufactured industrial machinery; Tom Hastings, sales manager of Minneapolis Brewery; advertising executive John Cornelius; and Mike Fadell.

The festival was conceived as a non-profit entity to be financed by business memberships, sponsorships, individual memberships, advertising revenue from brochures and souvenir booklets, the sale of Skipper Pins, and ticket sales to the Aqua Follies and other events. Most important of all, the businessmen who inaugurated the event envisioned that legions of committed volunteers would serve as the festival's backbone.

And that's how it turned out. Tom Hastings was elected President of the Aquatennial Association with W. R. "Win" Stephens, Sr. serving as the first Commodore. Both men were highly esteemed in the Minneapolis community, and they were a perfect team to bring national renown to the festival. A Board of Directors was formed and committees got to work organizing a variety of events. On the basis of handshakes, civic commitment, and lots of hard work, the city of Minneapolis accomplished the near-impossible. Less than a year after the idea was conceived, on July 20, 1940, the first Minneapolis Aquatennial got underway, and it was a smash. (Since 1940 the festival has always been held the third week of July because local weather forecasters consider that to be the driest, warmest week of the year. In 1940 the temperature soared to 103 degrees.)

The first Aquatennial competed for newspaper space with the Democratic National Convention, which nominated Franklin D. Roosevelt to an unprecedented third term, and with the assault of Hitler's Luftwaffe on England. The theme of that first Aquatennial was Where Life Begins At 40. Official nautical uniforms were designed as the traditional formal wear for the event, a tradition that continues to this day. The *Minneapolis Tribune* devoted twenty-three pages to the first festival.

More than 170 events were scheduled for that first action-packed festival, which ran for nine days. Early in the year, organizers held a city-wide contest to name their new creation. Minneapolis resident Rudolph G. Willer earned $50.00 for his entry "Aquatennial" which won out over such entries as "Fiestifete," "Lady of the Lakes Frolic," and "Aqualand Sun Party." The name was well-suited to a city with 147 parks, 22 lakes, and the mighty Mississippi running through it. The event was soon dubbed America's Greatest Summer Festival.

Among the activities staged during the first Aquatennial was the first Torchlight Parade, then called the Illuminated Evening Parade. A four-hour parade with eighty floats and fifty bands thrilled first time spectators. Several hundred mail carriers in uniform proudly marched in the parade. The St. Paul Winter Carnival sent a 500-person drum corps. Many downtown stores were closed during the parade time so no one would miss the extravaganza, the first of many to come.

13

14

Thrilling Air Show

See America's biggest and most thrilling 1940 air show at Wold-Chamberlain Field, July 26, 27 and 28, presenting more than a score of the nation's greatest flyers. Breath-catching aerobatics staged only twenty feet off the ground, and within 200 feet of the spectators, will be a top-notch feature. Thrilling races and stunt flying by internationally-famed pilots will hold tens of thousands spellbound. A gigantic exhibit of all types of planes by leading manufacturers will complete the program.

Championship Rodeo

See the only championship rodeo ever held in Minneapolis, presenting 300 saddle and bareback bucking broncos, Brahma bulls and catalo, and long-horned steers, and scores of the West's greatest riders, ropers, and bull-doggers, in red-blooded contests for national honors. Feature of the features will be Gene Autry, "The Singing Cowboy", and his wonder-horse, "Champion". A big village of Sioux, Gros Ventre and Arikaras Indians, in colorful tribal dances and pow-wows, will complete the picture.

"Over the Rainbow"

See the brilliant Auditorium Evening Stage Revue, "Over the Rainbow", presenting an enormous stage cast of dancers, singers, skaters and top-notch vaudeville artists from all parts of America. Novel scenic and lighting effects, elaborate and gorgeous costumes, and thrilling acts from New York, Chicago, Frisco and other cities will enthrall you. Two and a half hours of breath-taking entertainment will be climaxed by an inspiring finale, "America", in which the entire company of 200 will take part.

Spectacular Aqua Follies

See the colorful Aqua Follies, gorgeous evening water show at Cedar Lake, presenting dozens of famous divers, swimmers, acrobats and clowns, in spine-tingling exhibitions and contests. National indoor and outdoor men and women champions in Olympic-distance races and exciting contests will compete for prizes. A brilliant water ballet, featuring rhythmic swimming to music, will be staged by more than three dozen of the Northwest's most accomplished girl swimmers, specially trained for the event.

AFTER THE CEROMONIES *with* GENE AUTRY *and his* "ADOPTED" FAMILY

Gene Autry (opposite page, upper left and right) was the parade Grand Marshall and honored guest. At the time he was among America's most popular film and radio stars. He brought his horse Champion and the Melody Ranch Gang along with him, and stayed for the entire week of the festival.

Chief One Bull, then 92 years old, was also a special guest. He was Sitting Bull's nephew, and the last of the great Lakota warriors who had fought in the Battle of the Little Bighorn.

A rodeo was held at Parade Stadium for eight days, and an air show at Wold Chamberlain Field excited more than 100,000 viewers.

A water show, the precursor to the Aqua Follies, was held at Cedar Lake in 1940. More than 64,000 people attended during the course of the multi-day show. Maury Ostrander, clad in a gasoline soaked asbestos suit, did a handstand on the end of the diving board while an attendant applied a torch to his suit. He stood there a few seconds more before diving into the water, a veritable ball of flame. (For more on the Aqua Follies, see pp. 28-43.)

The St. Paul Winter Carnival had been revived in 1938, and civic leaders from that city provided valuable advice to the organizers of the Aquatennial in its early years. Here some of the Vulcans seem to be initiating a few Minneapolitans, including Dave Onan (back row, second from right).

Powderhorn Park, which has a natural amphitheatre (above), became the scene of Sunday interdenominational services. Aquatennial participants and Queen candidates attended what was called God's Outdoor Temple.

Minnesota's most famous woman golfer, Patty Berg (upper left), drew crowds in a special demonstration at Theodore Wirth Park. Archery contests and a regatta were also on the schedule.

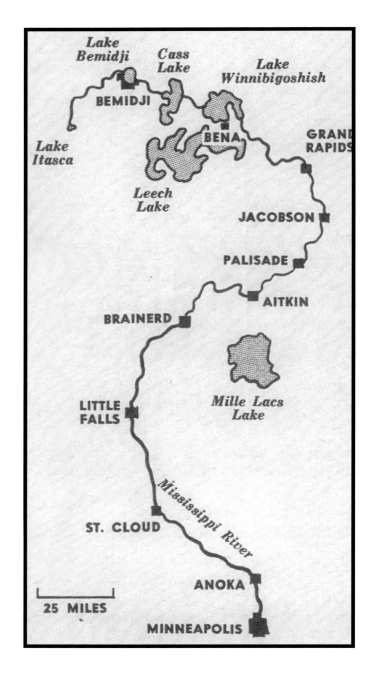

Lake Bemidji

Cass Lake

Lake Winnibigoshish

BEMIDJI

Lake Itasca

BENA

GRAND RAPIDS

Leech Lake

JACOBSON

PALISADE

AITKIN

BRAINERD

Mille Lacs Lake

LITTLE FALLS

Mississippi River

ST. CLOUD

ANOKA

25 MILES

MINNEAPOLIS

The Paul Bunyan Canoe Derby started in Bemidji and ended 450 miles downstream in Minneapolis. Teams of paddlers began training in April when the trees were still bare (opposite page). The trip took ten days and severely tested the strength, stamina, and whitewater skills of the two-person teams. The route was designed so that the winning team would arrive on the opening day of the festival. The first winners of the race (and recipients of the substantial $500 prize) were Ace and Ed Eliason, who finished the trip with a time of sixty-five hours. The last race was held in 1962.

The first festival featured small daily parades in neighborhoods throughout the city and four major parades full of glamour and fantasy. The Pageant of the Lakes was a three-mile water parade on Lake Calhoun with lighted floats, gondolas, canoes, and other watercraft. The extravaganza was followed by an hour of fireworks.

Music was also an important part of the first Aquatennial celebration. Mason Mallory, a Western Airlines executive, wrote the song "Minneapolis At Aquatennial Time" as the official festival theme song. It was later made popular by songstress Gail Farrell, a featured artist with the Lawrence Welk Show, and recorded by the Solidaires with the Red Wolfe Trio.

Another hit that year was the "Aquatennial Swing" with music by George Barton, Jr., leader of the dance orchestra then appearing at the Nicollet Hotel, and words by band-members Tommy McGovern and Oscar Hirsch. The song paid tribute to both the festival and the *Minneapolis Tribune* newspapers.

Greet your neighbor with a Rowdy
It's no time to frown, its Aquatennial town.
People come from many places
And we're always glad to see new faces.
Let them see you smile, happy all the while.
From coast to coast and sea to sea
From Oregon to Tennessee
All roads lead to Minneapolis.

They're coming here on Pullman trains.
They're flying here on aero planes.
They're coming to the Aquatennial
'Cause there'll be dancing, swimming
Just what the young folks do
Fishing and boating for the old folks too.
Bands will play as people sway
Crowds will shout hey-hey-hey
Let's go to the Aquatennial.
HeyHey

The directors and officials of the first Aquatennial in their natty new uniforms: in front row (from left) Algot Swanson, Walter Quist, Richard Kitchen, Tom Hastings (President), W. R. Stephens (Commodore), Henry Baker, Pat Carr , Ben Ferriss, and Arthur Randall. In back row (from left): George Murk, Earl Gammons, D. W. Onan, Tom Palmer, Tom Von Kuster, William Benson, George Adams, John Cornelius, Neil Messick, John Friedl, and Mike Fadell. This get-together at the Nicollet Hotel followed several earlier planning sessions.

From the first, the Aquatennial relied on the efforts of an extraordinary group of volunteers. Three hundred people showed up at an organizational meeting held at the West Hotel in February 1940. "That was the worst day I've ever had," said Tom Hastings, the event's first President, "but also the most encouraging. People wanted to help."

The *Minneapolis Tribune* devoted twenty three pages of copy and photos acquainting readers with the splendors of the new festival and its attractions. And starting at noon every day during the festival, 490 fountains on the north shore of Lake Calhoun known as the Lagoon of Fountains, played and sprayed their Aqua magic. At 8:00 p.m., 800 colored lamps were lit until midnight, making a visual orchestra of light.

The Aqua Trot

In an effort to get communities throughout the state involved, organizers arranged with nine mid-sized towns along the Paul Bunyan Canoe Derby route to hold regional dance competitions, and sent them mimeographed diagrams of the basic steps to a new dance created expressly for the occasion: the Aqua Trot. Dancers at the Excelsior and Marigold ballrooms in Minneapolis also enrolled in the competition.

Winners of these regional and local competitions convened on Nicollet Avenue for the final showdown and street dance on July 23. Three blocks of the street were closed, streetcars were rerouted, the street was cleaned, and a ton of borax was spread around to improve the gliding surface. Then more than 10,000 men and women trotted down Nicollet Avenue performing the dance, which was basically a simple "shag" step interspersed with random actions purporting to be interpretations of any Minnesota sport.

The first Aquatennial competed for newspaper space with the Democratic National Convention and with the assault of Hitler's Luftwaffe on England. It also played host to the National Outboard Races on Lake Calhoun; more that a hundred thousand attended.

Minneapolis TIMES TRIBUNE

WEATHER Partly cloudy tonight and Sunday, not quite so warm tonight. 24-hour high. 100; year ago high, 85; noon today, 90. Details on page 5.

4

Saturday Evening, July 20, 1940
16 Pages. Two Cents in Minneapolis
SEVENTY-FOURTH YEAR. NO. 57

German Bombers Blast at Britain Again in Worst Air Raid of War

Loop Jammed for Aqua Parade

Normal Business Virtually Halts As Festival Opens

Anoka Crowds Watch Derby

'Batman' Is Missing After Plane Jump

Toll of Civilian Deaths Reaches 336 in Month

Belief Grows That Hitler Will Launch Invasion Within Few Days—Nazi Radio Tries to Arouse Distrust of Leaders in British Public

By THE ASSOCIATED PRESS

After the United States entered the war late in 1941, civic leaders discussed whether it was appropriate to continue holding the Aquatennial. They decided the festival was a great boost to civilian morale. During the 1942 Aquatennial, 400,000 people saw the patriotic "On to Victory" parade, with representatives of the Army, Navy, Marines, and Coast Guard taking center stage. After the war a number of events, including the polo matches and the rodeo, were eliminated.

Queen of the Lakes

The first Aquatennial Queen, Eva Brunson, enjoys a few words with two of the festival's founding fathers, Win Stephens and Tom Hastings, at the Mayor's Day Luncheon held at the Grain Belt Brewery.

Joyce Moen (left) was chosen first Aquatennial Queen of the Lakes, but she relinquished her crown to be married, and Eva Brunson assumed the role. Eva is considered historically to be the first queen, because she was the first to reign over the festival. Beautiful inside and out, she was revered by the queens who followed her.

Queens of the 1940s

Vivian Hofstad

Barbara Matson

Patty Carlson

Nancy Thom

Marilyn Lindstrom

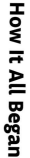
Ruth Tolman

Patty McLane

Lee Jeanson

Over the years a variety of crowns and dresses were designed for Aquatennial Queens. This dress (left), worn by 1948 Queen Patty McLane, was created by her sponsor, Dayton's Department Store. It's an exact duplicate of Queen Elizabeth's wedding dress.

Young women selected in their home cities throughout the state arrived in Minneapolis to vie for the honor of being chosen Queen of the Lakes. In 1947 Ruth Tolman of St. Cloud (bottom row, seated, fifth from the left) was the winner.

Ruth Tolman (1947)

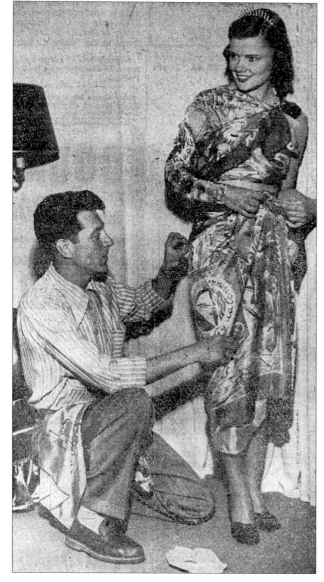

Lee Jaenson (1949) getting fitted in her Aquatennial scarf dress.

Serving as Aquatennial Queen had its responsibilities...and also its perks.

In 1946, the Aquatennial's first water ski show was introduced at Lake Calhoun. That same year, the floats in the Torchlight Parade drew on a hundred thousand watts of power to lend a dazzling illumination to the night.

Also in 1946 the Aqua Jesters were formed—a group of one hundred business and professional men, artisans, students, and laborers whose hobby was, and remains, to make others happy. Throughout the years, they have appeared in civic parades across the state, as well as enlivening the numerous Aquatennial parades annually. Original costumes, clever gags, and down-right deviltry make these businessmen unsurpassed in the art of fun.

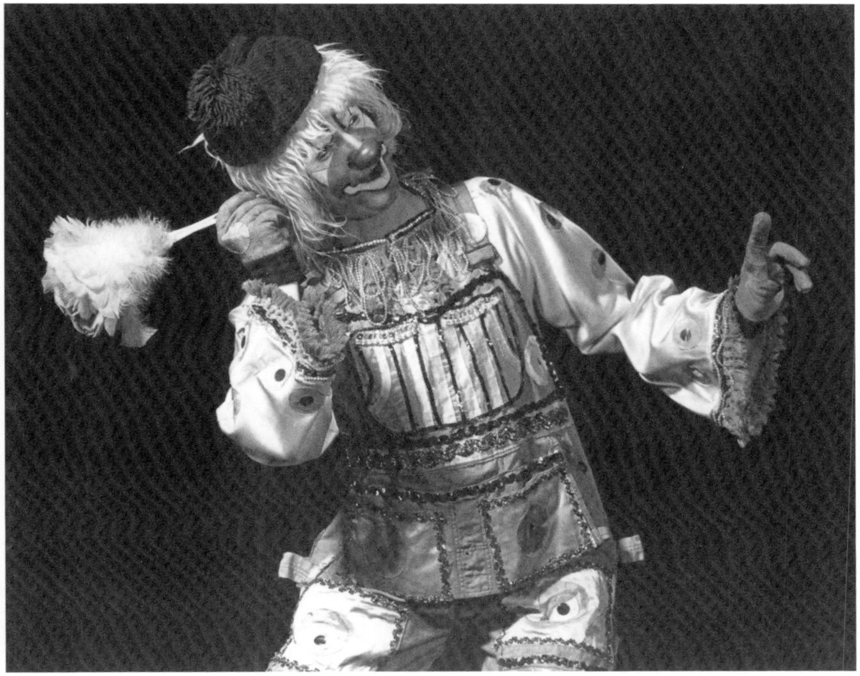

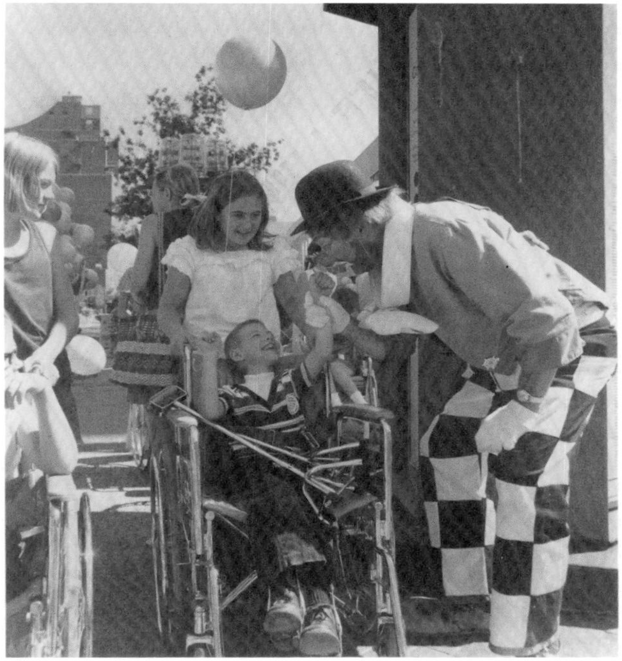

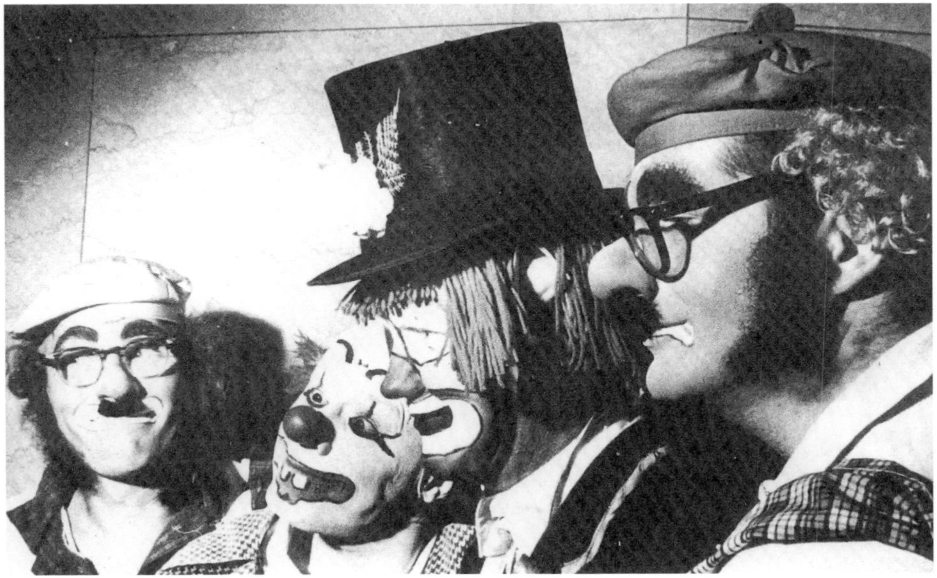

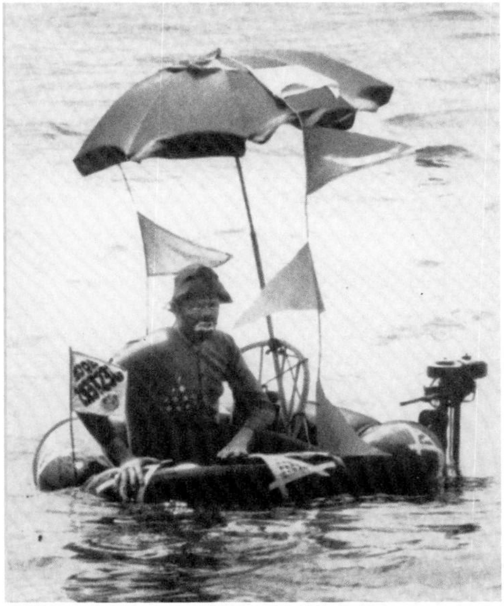

From the first, local businesses were eager to contribute to the success of the Aquatennial. In 1947, for example, the owner of Mabel's Chapeau Salon (1903 E. Lake Street) designed the new bronze sequin crown for Queen Ruth Tolmen (shown at left). That same year, the fifty-thousandth car to roll off the assembly line of the Minnesota Ford plant was donated to the event to serve as the Queen's parade car. In 1948 the craftsmen at Dayton-Hudson Corp. designed a new crown (see photo below) for Queen Patty McLane. It served as the official coronation crown for years. That same year a stunning Oldsmobile convertible was donated by Malkerson Sales, Inc., of Shakopee, to serve as the Queen's offical car.

RUTH TOLMAN
Queen of the Lakes
COURTESY
Ford Motor Co.

In 1948 a Junior Royalty program was introduced to the Aquatennial. Carolyn Rose Herrmann was crowned first Junior Royalty Queen. The juniors were referred to as "the dimple in Aqua cheeks" or "our pint sized royalty." Bridge tournaments were also added to the festival, attracting competitors from around the state.

A new rose called the Queen of the Lakes was developed, and thousands of game fish were released into Lake Calhoun so Minneapolis youngsters could follow the summer advice, "Hey, Skinney, let's go fishing!" A Fish Derby for girls and boys under fifteen years of age was held and a plethora of prizes were awarded to those who had the best luck.

A miniature replica of the skipper wheel of the *USS Minnesota* was added to the Skipper Pin sailing logo in 1948, and as usual, a Twelfth Night Aquatennial Christmas Tree Bonfire was held in early January 1949 under the co-sponsorship of the Minneapolis Junior Chamber of Commerce. This annual event served as a fire prevention measure, helping to rid the city of tinder-dry Christmas trees—people around the city dropped off their trees at the Parade park just west of downtown. But the bonfire event was also a very festive occasion tied to the traditional Twelfth Night celebration ending the Christmas season. The bonfire itself provided a spectacular display that attracted thousands to the Parade annually. It also signaled the beginning of a new Aquatennial year.

A Twelfth Night Aquatennial Christmas Tree Bonfire was held in early January 1949.

During the 1948 festival, Smorgy, a cartoon character created by Kurt Carlson that appeared in the *Minneapolis Tribune*, had a severe crush on Queen Patty McLane, though his attentions were rebuffed repeatedly.

Above: By the late forties, the Harmony Ambassadors had begun to entertain audiences at festival functions, and they were an Aquatennial mainstay right up to the 1970s. The group consisted of Theodore (Choppy) Kline, tenor; Paul L. Behrend, tenor; Joe F. Williams, baritone; Robert E. Anderson, basso; and Clem Borland, baritone.

Left: During WWII, a stiff excise tax on clubs where dancing was allowed put a damper on some forms of nightlife. After the war, the Jitterbug burst into full swing.

The Aquatennial in 1949 chose as its theme the founding of Minnesota Territory one hundred years earlier, and Mary Dure, the queen of the state's Centennial Celebration, was the featured Aqua guest. But the festival was launched with an unrelated event—the world premiere of the movie *Dan Patch*, which chronicled the career of the world-famous horse by that name, a pacer, who held the world speed record for many years. The horse was owned by Marion Savage, a local entrepeneur who built his stock feed company into a international success by shrewdly associating his products with the health and prowess of his talented steed.

Adding to the retrospective flavor of the year's festivities, the University of Minnesota staged a pageant on the state's history in conjunction with the Minnesota Territorial Centennial Commission at the U's Memorial Stadium.

A hundred antique automobiles dating back to 1896 appeared in the Grande Parade, and Dayton's sponsored a float depicting episodes in Minnesota's history that was 125 feet long. U.S. Vice President Alben W. Barkley was the honored Grand Marshall for the Grande Day Parade.

Aquatennial organizers sponsored the first "Radio Day" in 1949, inviting forty-one station owners and their guests to join in a specially arranged day of festival events. Twelve bands roamed the city streets during the Aquatennial to serenade passersby. They were especially popular in front of the city's seven major hotels: the Andrews, Curtis, Dyckman, Leamington, Normandy, Radisson, and Pick-Nicollet.

Dave Onan, one of the festival founders, was Treasurer for the festival's first nine years, and his skills helped to insuring its continuing success. It was said he could make 1 + 1 = 4 when needed.

On the first day of the inaugural Aquatennial, back in 1940, rain had threatened, and the Aquatennial's first President, Tom Hastings, had asked the Little Sisters of the Poor to pray for good weather. The prayers

Above: Carol Rose Herrmann, age 4, was chosen from among 356 children to be the first Junior Queen.

were answered. A similar situation arose in 1949, and once again the Little Sisters were called into action. Miraculously, the sun came out again.

In 1940, 61,369 Skipper Pins were sold for $1.00 each. The first pins were made of celluloid-covered steel. During WWII celluloid was difficult to come by, so in 1943 no pins were produced. Instead, a paper tag resembling a shipping label was used. These are almost impossible to find today. Plastic Skipper Pins came into use in 1955. In 1948 a miniature replica of the skipper wheel of the USS Minnesota was added to the Skipper Pin sailing logo.

the Aqua Follies

When the Aquatennial was organized in 1940, the founders were convinced a summer water festival needed a major water event to become an annual extravaganza, and a huge party with a style show was staged at Cedar Lake. The event didn't really take off, how-ever, until the following year, when the venue was changed to Wirth Lake, just west of down-town Minneapolis, and veteran showman Al Sheehan, Minneapolis's Mr. Showbiz, was hired to produce it. Sheehan had seen the Billy Rose Aquacade at the 1939-1940 New York World's Fair and was inspired. He knew he could design a similar water show that would be more spectacular than anything ever seen before in the Upper Midwest.

The Aquatennial Association contracted with Sheehan to bring in aquatic stars, Olympic divers, and a stage show production for added glamour. Theodore Wirth Lake had the natural setting he was envisioning for his production. Work began dredging the underwater muck and putting in pilings and walls to achieve the 42x110x15-foot dimensions. Two 33-foot diving platforms was constructed as well as a grandstand where capacity crowds of 6,000 gathered for matinee or evening spectaculars throughout the Aquatennial's ten-day schedule. An elaborate stage with hidden lighting and a grand staircase added to the impact. Eventually matinees were discontinued because audiences preferred night shows when the lights, reflected in the waters, created splendid fantasy. The Aqua-Follies almost immediately became one of the leading moneymakers for the festival.

The first year in the new stadium a traveling water ballet was hired to do the show. Morton Downy, Sr. was the Master of Ceremonies. A local stage ballet company was hired as well as a band. Later Burt Hanson replaced Morton Downy as the annual MC; he soon became the Voice of the Aqua Follies. The show was so popular in 1941 that it was held over another week.

Sheehan was averse to introducing new songs to the shows. He believed using the same songs would capture the audiences year after year. He also insisted on tight scripts and perfect timing to insure that the show would be exactly two hours long.

Al Sheehan (right), the producer of Aqua Follies, confers with stage manager Fred Smith on a scale model of Theodore Wirth pool about details of an upcoming Chinese-themed number.

Precision swimmers called the Aqua Belles (and later the Aqua Dears), diving exhibitions, illuminated water exhibitions, comedy routines, and lavish dancing productions by the group known as the Aqua Darlings were featured at every show. Olympic and professional divers such as Charlie Diehl, Hobie Billingsly, Orwin Harvey, and Joaquin Capilla thrilled capacity crowds with their daredevil dives off three-, five-, and ten-meter boards into fifteen feet of water.

Many early production costumes had been used in Broadway plays; they were rented from Madame Bertha's in New York City. Others came from Hollywood costume houses. The Aqua Dears were required to be 125 pounds and stand five feet, four inches tall. Helen

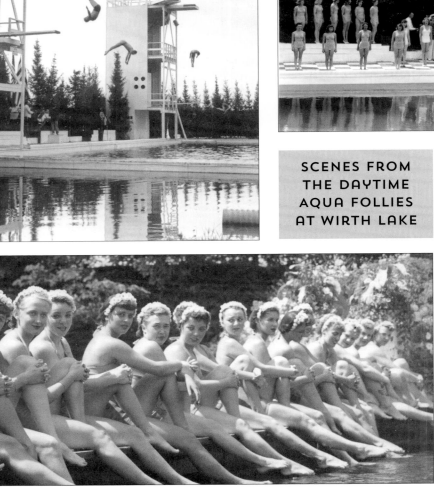

SCENES FROM
THE DAYTIME
AQUA FOLLIES
AT WIRTH LAKE

The Aqua Dears (left), the water ballet troupe of the Aqua Follies, were all recruited from Minnesota, though the star performers were often national celebrities like Lynn Paulson (above).

Starr, Associate Professor of Physical Education at the University of Minnesota, was the no-nonsense director of the meticulously rehearsed water ballets. The results were always a work of art. This rhythmic, precision swimming group of no more than 24 young ladies exhibited strength and stamina while performing intricate water movements in synchronized formations, swimming, diving,

and manipulating bulky props. They also had to concentrate on keeping their legs moving at all times and to avoid touching the sides of the pool, even in practice or if a snapping turtle happened to introduce himself underwater. The idea was to strengthen their legs as much as possible. The performers also had to carefully maneuver the underwater cables used in the productions.

The Aqua Dears had four swimsuits apiece designed by Rose Marie Reid and Jantzen. Each night the suits were washed to extract chlorine. All swimmers had to clean their ears nightly with alcohol to prevent water bacteria build-up and ear infections.

Fred Smith, Stage and Water Property Designs Manager, was responsible for construction sites and the building of special effects. The props were made with Solastic by Dupont, a cloth impregnated with a plastic substance to make them waterproof papier-

Daredevil stunt-diver Orwin Harvey (right) joined the Aqua Follies in 1953 after performing in similar water shows in Las Vegas, Palm Springs, and Lake Tahoe. He entertained audiences with his crazy bathing suits and also his vast repertoire of flops, flips, and cannonballs, executed from great heights.

Joaquin Capilla (below) won an Olympic diving medal for Mexico in 1956 and went on to a stellar career as a professional diver for the Aqua Follies and other troupes.

Charlie Diehl, "the world heavyweight champion of the high boards," thrilled audiences at Wirth pool every summer for nearly twenty years.

The Aqua Follies water ballet (left) was traditionally made up of young women from the Upper Midwest. The stage ballet (above) was composed almost entirely of professional dancers from other parts of the country.

mâché. Among his most spectacular water floats were a ten-foot-tall Eiffel Tower replica with thousands of tiny lights, a menagerie of Asian paraphernalia that Al Sheehan went to China to research, and a reproduction of the Taj Mahal that Fred created to exact proportions.

Bachman's florists installed pine trees for each year's scenic backdrop and to hide the ramps leading to the dressing rooms under the grandstand. In many years the beautiful setting hosted the Queen of the Lakes coronation.

Copper sulphate was used to clean the pool each day. The site was sprayed with DDT every afternoon at 3:00 to control mosquitoes. Every spring divers were hired to pick up props, cans, broken glass, and other items that had accumulated on the bottom of the pool.

By the early 1960s, the swimming pool, the two wooden diving platforms, and the grandstand, were in need of major repairs, but funding was not forthcoming. In the summer of 1964, the famous Aqua Follies gave its final performances. The diving towers and grandstand were demolished, and the water in the swimming pool given back to the lake.

Along with the two magical Aquatennial parades, the Aqua Follies was the most eagerly anticipated event of the festival. This lavishly produced spectacle was unrivaled in its time. What remains are fragile souvenirs and photos in old scrapbooks, though a small kiosk stands forlornly on the southeast shore of Wirth Lake to mark the original Follies site. To those who were there, it may hauntingly evoke memories of music wafting over the lake as families gathered on hot summer evenings to enjoy a watery spectacle under the romantic night sky.

The suspense leading up to the selection of the new Queen of the Lakes is exhilarating, somewhat akin to an out-of-body experience. As the Commodore walks up to one young woman, he salutes her, indicating "she is the one." Immediately she feels the sensations of floating in a dream-like state, thrilled but frightened at this immediate new reality and enormous responsibility that is now hers. She has been chosen as a public relations ambassador representing a great civic legacy, the Minneapolis Aquatennial.

Clockwise from upper left: Linda Kleinert (1966), Connie Haenny (1963), Amanda Bertrand (2012), Betty Trones (1954).
Opposite page: Ruth Tolman (1947).

Jennifer Tolrud (1988) being helped by the previous year's Queen Sandra Polesky

Being crowned Queen is a life-altering moment, as a talented but relatively unknown young woman begins a year-long whirlwind of royal protocol. She has suddenly become a royal ambassador of America's Greatest Summer Festival—a festival that signifies excitement, community, pomp and pageantry, colorful events, exhilerating competitions, musical entertainment, water sports, celebrities, and the glory of Minneapolis and Minnesota. In that one moment in time, she has become the guardian of the revered Aquatennial traditions.

For decades the Aquatennial Queens were ranked among the most traveled Queens in the United States, second only to Miss America. In the mid-50s through the late 80s, Aquatennial Queens traveled more than 125,000 miles and made more than 500 appearances at pageants, parades, and local festivals throughout Minnesota. Among the Minnesota festivals Aquatennial Queens and Princesses have participated in are:

St. Paul Winter Carnival
Montevideo Fiesta Days
Cokato Corn Festival
Granite Falls Festival on Main
Glenwood Waterama

Anoka Halloween Fest
Willmar Fests
Hopkins Raspberry Festival
Robbinsdale Whiz Bang Days
Maple Grove Days
Clara City Prairie Fest Celebration
Northfield's Defeat of Jesse James Days
Rockford Harvest Fest
Winona Steamboat Days
Delano 4th of July
New Brighton Stockyard Days
Hutchinson Jaycees Water Carnival

Additionally, as honored guests, the Royal Party has, throughout the years, brought the glory and grandeur of Aquatennial and Minnesota to prestigious festivals throughout the United States.

Portland Parade of Roses
Seattle World's Fair
Sarasota Buccaneer Days
Corpus Christi Buccaneer Days
St. Petersburg Sunshine Festival
Chicago Musicland Festival
San Antonio Fiesta Flambeau
Mobile Azalea Festival
Pasadena Tournament of Roses
Aberdeen Snow Festival
Macon Cherry Blossom Festival
La Crosse Oktoberfest
El Paso Sun Bowl
Burlington, Carolina Carousel Festival
Washington, D.C. Cherry Blossom Festival

Bismarck Folk Fest
Austin Aqua Fest
Billings Go Western Rodeo
Memphis Great River Festival
Spokane Lilac Festival
Tampa Latin America Festival
Anchorage Fur Rendezvous
Fairbanks Ice Bowl

The Queen of the Lakes has also made waves around the world, extending Minnesota's good-will to foreign destinations on tours sometimes lasting as long as three weeks. Among the scheduled visits have been Winnipeg, Calgary, Rio, Brasilia, Montevideo, Sao Paulo, Caracas, Buenos Aires, Lima, Paris, London, Hong Kong, Bangkok, Seoul, Osaka, Okinawa, Tahiti, and various cities in the Netherlands, Germany, Austria, Finland, Denmark, Sweden, Russia, New Zealand, and the Caribbean.

Queen Marlene Dolbec (1955) tells members of the Italian press corps in Rome about the Minneapolis Aquatennial and Minnesota.

Barbara Flanagan with Queen Joanne Melberg (1952) in Oslo.

Barbara Flanagan served for many years as chaperone for the Queens during their overseas trips. She later described in a reminsicence being driven down a bobsped track in a small French car with Queen Joanne Melberg (pictured above), and meeting Coco Chanel at a photo shoot she'd arranged for Queen Gail Nygaard (1960) at Chanel in Paris. Queen Judy Penny actually took a bullfighting lesson in Spain, which might not have been a good idea, but in the end no one got hurt.

In each decade Aquatennial Queens—and since the 1950s the Princesses, too—have reflected the prevailing mindset of women and their images. The 40s were Norman Rockwell Americana and the economy of the war; the 50s brought us into crinolines and poodle skirts, rock and roll and *Father Knows Best*. The 60s saw an end to the illusion of Donna Reed and Camelot, thereby liberating women to catapult themselves into the business suits and bow-ties of the 70s. The 80s brought an era of "can-do candor" which empowered the technocrat women of the nineties and an increasing array of evolving female roles of the twenty-first century.

Every festival Queen and Princess would agree that the experience has played a significant role in her perspectives and choices in life. The scrapbooks and tiaras are now packed away, but the memories are as vivid as yesterday. We extend our sincere gratitude for the gift of that "one brief moment in time" when we were each the proud ambassador of service to our revered festival. The splendor of the Aquatennial is matched by the joy of the lifelong family of friends that live lovingly in our hearts and memories.

May the Aquatennial traditions and pageantry and "hands across the world" continue to reign supreme as a cherished piece of Americana.

"It truly was a dazzling dream!"

Gloria Haberl
Golden Valley

Betty Stemper
School of Engineering

Pat Patter
Mpls-Richfield Legion Post 435

Bonita Johnson
Hopkins Raspberry Queen

Rita Bachynsky
Scott-Atwater Mfg. Co.

Ann Allard
Northwestern Bell Telephone

Some Queen Candidates from the early 1950s

Candidates for 2009 Queen of the Lakes: You be the judge!

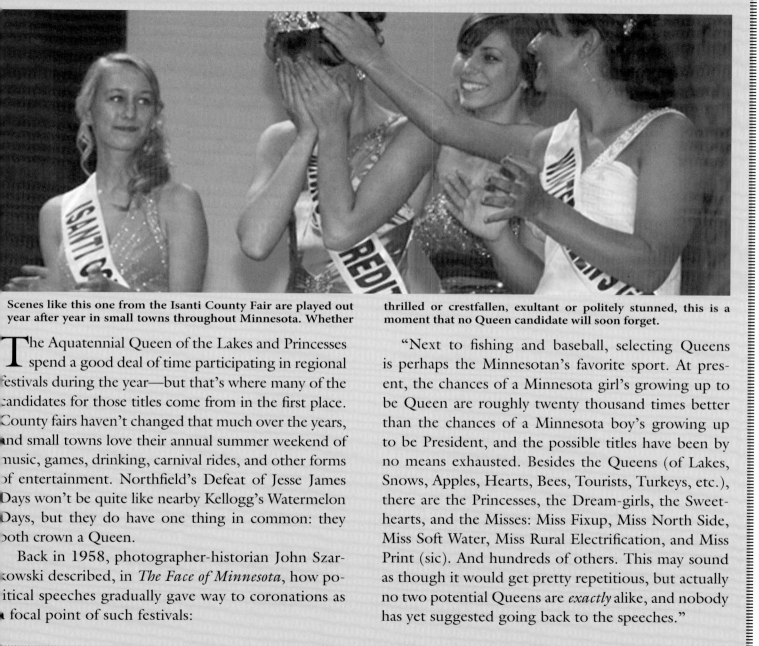

Scenes like this one from the Isanti County Fair are played out year after year in small towns throughout Minnesota. Whether thrilled or crestfallen, exultant or politely stunned, this is a moment that no Queen candidate will soon forget.

The Aquatennial Queen of the Lakes and Princesses spend a good deal of time participating in regional festivals during the year—but that's where many of the candidates for those titles come from in the first place. County fairs haven't changed that much over the years, and small towns love their annual summer weekend of music, games, drinking, carnival rides, and other forms of entertainment. Northfield's Defeat of Jesse James Days won't be quite like nearby Kellogg's Watermelon Days, but they do have one thing in common: they both crown a Queen.

Back in 1958, photographer-historian John Szarkowski described, in *The Face of Minnesota*, how political speeches gradually gave way to coronations as a focal point of such festivals:

"Next to fishing and baseball, selecting Queens is perhaps the Minnesotan's favorite sport. At present, the chances of a Minnesota girl's growing up to be Queen are roughly twenty thousand times better than the chances of a Minnesota boy's growing up to be President, and the possible titles have been by no means exhausted. Besides the Queens (of Lakes, Snows, Apples, Hearts, Bees, Tourists, Turkeys, etc.), there are the Princesses, the Dream-girls, the Sweethearts, and the Misses: Miss Fixup, Miss North Side, Miss Soft Water, Miss Rural Electrification, and Miss Print (sic). And hundreds of others. This may sound as though it would get pretty repetitious, but actually no two potential Queens are *exactly* alike, and nobody has yet suggested going back to the speeches."

"AMERICA'S GREATEST SUMMER FESTIVAL"

By the time the Minneapolis Aquatennial entered its second decade, many of its routines had become well-established. But every year, popular events were given a new twist, activities were added and others were removed.

In 1950, the Aquatennial parades were televised by WCCO for the first time. The festival also played host to a national grand slam bridge tournament that year, and promotors began to use a new festival slogan:

AMERICA'S GREATEST SUMMER FESTIVAL

Life magazine devoted a full-page color ad to the Aquatennial in its July 24, 1950, issue. And Queen of the Lakes Jean Johnson was featured in a Sunday *Tribune* article called "Paper Doll," pictured as a beautiful paper doll accompanied with clothes that readers could cut out to style her.

That year the Minnesota Apparel Industries presented a new royal robe (shown at right on Queen Betty Barnhart) to Queen of the Lakes Jean Johnson. Designed by Kickernick Company artists, it was fashioned by the Paramount Coat Company. The floor-length white cape was embroidered with aqua beads in an "Aqua" motif. It was an exquisite complement to the official 1948 coronation crown!

Queen Jean flew Western Airlines to Denver on an inaugural, non-stop flight that introduced DC-4's to the growing mountain city.

In 1950 new "avenue of pennants" decorations were purchased and installed on Nicollet Avenue (opposite page) making the festival week even more celebratory.

Queen of the Lakes Betty Barnhart (1952)

Among the aquatic events of 1952 was a water-skiing show on Lake Calhoun and a series of daily speedboat races along the Mississippi from Grand Rapids to Minneapolis. The canoe race down the river had been dropped due to lack of interest, but the response to the outboard races was lukewarm, and they, too, were soon discontinued.

In 1950 a young man named Norton Stillman won the seventh annual Aquatennial Conservation Essay Contest. Today he is the publisher of this book and many other fine regional titles.

Construction had begun on Parade Stadium, located just west of the park now occupied by the Walker Sculpture Garden, in 1950. Intended to be a venue for football games and other athletic events, the stadium was largely completed by the following summer. The first major event hosted there was a childrens' Aquatennial event at which the Lone Ranger and his horse, Silver, appeared. For many years thereafter Parade Stadium served as the starting point of the two major Aquatennial parades each summer.

The stadium had parking for 1,000 vehicles and seating for 20,000 spectators. Marching bands and lavish floats would promenade around the stadium during the Grande Day and Torchlight Parades before moving on to Nicollet Avenue to entertain the throngs of excited parade-goers who lined the streets.

Musical performances and competitions have always been an important part of the Aquatennial festivities. The solo vocal contest of 1954 offered an impressive selection of operatic arias by Verdi, Puccini, Mozart, Gluck, Wagner, and other greats. Meanwhile, choral groups such as the Carillon Singers (above), under the direction of Edith Byquist Norberg, entertained audiences for the fourth straight year.

Gloriane Oldin (right) took first place in the Chicagoland Music Festival in 1953 to become Class A National Accordion Champion. She was especially pleased at the result: she'd had to settle for second place at the Aquatennial competition earlier that year.

In 1959 the festival introduced a Hawaiian Review led by hula-expert Nona Beamer (above right), in honor of Hawaii's entry into the United States earlier that year.

Throughout the 40's and 50's media journalists Bob DeHaven and Cedric Adams (pictured above), along with George Grim and Howard Viken, were major supporters of the Aquatennial on radio, television, and in print. They also served as masters of ceremonies for many coronations. Adams had several columns in the *Minneapolis Star* paper, and he did more than fifty radio shows and eight television shows a week. It was said he needed seven secretaries to keep up with his fan mail. George Grim was a globetrotting journalist, radio and TV personality known for his *Minneapolis Tribune* column, "I Like it Here." Bob DeHaven personified the "good neighbor" spirit captured in his "Good Neighbor" radio show on WCCO. He was with the station for 25 years. In one way or another, all of these men became Midwestern media legends.

The 50s

In the early years of the Aquatennial, celebrities were invited to participate in the festival every year. Gene Autry, the Singing Cowboy, spent eight days at the festival in 1940. In subsequent years celebrities often came for a specific ceremony. Radio personalities such as Jack Benny were big, as were movie stars such as Minnesota's own Arlene Dahl. As TV became a familiar presence in the home, now-forgotten stars such as Garry Moore were invited to attend, along with youth idols like Mouseketeer Annette Funicello. Big Band leaders such as Paul Whiteman and Woody Herman were always a draw.

Clockwise from upper left: Home-town-girl Arlene Dahl; Bob Hope with Aquatennial Queen Lee Jaenson (1949); Mahalia Jackson; Cedric Adams with Arthur Godfrey singing "Aquatennial Time."

ckwise from upper left: Dave Garroway and Helen O'Connell; Art Linkletter
Jack Carson; Woody Herman; Garry Moore (who got rained on during the
chlight Parade); Jazz vocalists Lambert, Henricks, and Ross; Eddie Fisher with
star-struck Aqua princesses, Barbara Theilen and Sheila Boyle.

The 50s

A good deal of suspense surrounded the selection of the new Queen of the Lakes each year. Here Commodore Emmett L. Duemke struts back and forth in front of the candidates with a scroll in hand bearing the name of the winner. (It was Joanne Melberg.) Beginning in 1951, two Princesses were also chosen to be part of the Royal Party each year.

The Commodore for 1953, Neil Messick, Jr., later recalled: "My memory of 1953's Aquatennial is especially positive, not just because I had a most wonderful, bright, and well spoken Queen, Joanne Melberg, but also because we made a profit. Our year finished in the black thanks to a careful board of directors and President Bill Benson's banking skills."

Jean Johnson

Helen Jane Stoffer

Betty Barnhart

Joanne Melberg

Betty Trones

Marlene Dolbec

Judy Penny

Mary Erickson

Pat Wilson

Sharon Bigalke

Following the coronation ceremony a Coronation Ball was held at the Minneapolis Auditorium.

Left: The first Junior Commodore Greg Johnson with Junior Queen Suzanne Polkey

One of the Aquatennial's many roving units that traveled the metropolitan area and throughout the state to provide entertainment

In 1953, Loring Park was the scene of the Aqua-Hop dance. Twenty-five visiting queens from around the U.S. were honored guests of the royal party for a weeklong stay. More than 210,000 Skipper Pins were mailed to householders in Minneapolis and the surrounding suburbs, along with a card to facilitate the return of $.25. Another 90,000 Skippers were sent out to organizations and concessionaires to be sold at the same reduced price.

That same year, milkmen from Minneapolis and surrounding areas proudly sold the 1953 Skipper Pins for $1.00 with proceeds going towards purchases of iron lungs for polio victims.

Parade organizers limited the number of convertibles to be used for Queen candidates, feeling that having them on floats gave the parades more pizzazz. Queen of the Lakes Joanne Melberg's float got an extra shot of pizzazz when it started on fire in the staging area just prior to the parade. Quick action on the part of parade volunteers saved it just in time.

More than 450 Minnesota mayors, legislators, and their wives attended the annual Mayors and Legislators' Day program, which included an elegant luncheon, various afternoon events, a sumptuous dinner in the company of the the Queen candidates, and choice seats at Parade Stadium to watch the Torchlight Parade. No wonder the event was so well attended!

Some 300 newspaper editors and their wives were similarly entertained during Editors' Day, which took place annually on the first Saturday of the festival.

The Minneapolis Symphony, with the world-renowned conductor Antal Dorati at the podium, was featured at the Queen Coronation in 1954, fronted by Marguerite Piazza, a soprano who had sung with the

Metropolitan Opera but was better known as a night club entertainer. (She later appeared in the half-time show of Superbowl IV.) Among the featured selections was an official song dedicated to the newly crowned Queen, Betty Trones from Richfield, Minnesota.

Mel Hatling, veteran chairman of Aquatennial's Roving Units program, and his wife, Betty, worked diligently year after year to sponsor the groups. It was a tradition of promoting the festival throughout the city, suburbs, and state. Scores of talented entertainers from the metropolitan area gained valuable on-stage experience while performing a vital public service. Auditions allowed amateur performers to compete as singles and in groups. Dancers, singers, instrumental soloists, and instrumental groups were equally welcome. Each June they brought musical entertainment to shut-ins in hospitals and correctional institutions, and also performed at shopping centers and local festivals throughout the state.

That same year, Clarabell the Clown (Howdy Doody's sidekick) performed at Powderhorn Park to throngs of excited children, and a hundred cyclists from thirty states competed at Parade Stadium in the National Amateur Bicycle Championship Races. The Aqua Cruiser Classic, a non-stop cruiser trip from Minneapolis to New Orleans, captured the hearts of fans up and down the river who wildly cheered as the flotilla moved south.

In 1955 the Naval Air Cadets Choir from Pensac-

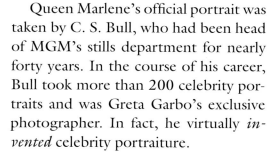

Queen of the Lakes Marlene Dolbec as rendered by C.S. Bull.

ola, Florida, made their second visit to the festival to escort Queen candidates and serenade the new Queen, Marlene Dolbec. Suzanne Polkey was crowned Junior Queen to reign with Junior Commodore Gregory Johnson. This was the first year Aquatennial choose a Junior Commodore. And also the first year that plastic Skipper Pins were sold.

Queen Marlene's official portrait was taken by C. S. Bull, who had been head of MGM's stills department for nearly forty years. In the course of his career, Bull took more than 200 celebrity portraits and was Greta Garbo's exclusive photographer. In fact, he virtually *invented* celebrity portraiture.

The following year a new Aquatennial theme song was introduced, with words and music by V. Arthur Koivumki. It was called "MINN-MINN-MINN-MINNE-A-PO-LIS, Minn." A new Aquatennial film was also released, with an equally straighforward title: *Aqua Film Around The World*. It made more than six hundred showings throughout the nation and was also screened in Japan and Sweden. It was filmed in color by General Mills and narrated by Minneapolis *Morning Tribune* columnist George Grim.

In honor of Minneapolis's centennial year, Queen of the Lakes Judy Penney sealed a Century vault that was then dropped to the bottom of Theodore Wirth Lake. The time capsule contained microfilmed stories of the

Above: Jayne Mansfield made a splash at the 1957 festival.

Below: Commodore Ellsworth Johnson, Queen Pat Wilson, and Senator Edward Thye invited Vice President Nixon to serve as Grand Marshall of the 1958 Aquatennial day parade. (Nixon accepted.)

achievements of one hundred Minneapolis businesses. (It might still be down there!)

That year Navy Frogmen from Pensacola, Florida, demonstrated underwater demolition tactics at Lake Calhoun, and Billy Graham conducted a less explosive interdenominational service at Parade Stadium which was heard on more than nine hundred radio stations in the U.S. and Canada and seventeen countries overseas via short wave.

In 1957 Bernice Stuart became the first woman to wear the Aquatennial uniform as committee chair for the Junior Royalty. TV personality Bob Barker's show, *Truth or Consequences*, was broadcast live from the Garden Court of newly opened Southdale Mall.

Mary Erickson, the 1958 Queen of the Lakes, was the first to be invited to appear in the Pasadena Tournament of Roses parade. From 1961 through 1986, the Queen of the Lakes rode in the Rose Parade every year.

Two popular national television shows thrilled local audiences with local appearances that year—Dave Garroway's *The Today Show* and *The Don McNeill Breakfast Club*. Participants were chosen from the audience for both shows.

An AAU Swimming and Diving competition was held at the municipal pool in Edina that year as part of the Aquatennial. And Hollywood's Million Dollar Mermaid, Esther Williams, was Grand Marshal, though she didn't appear as part of the Aqua Follies because her fee was too high.

All the same, the Aqua Follies continued to thrill crowds with its diving stars, precision water ballet, comic divers, swimming stars, and a star-studded stage show

The 1958 Queen of the Lakes, Sharon Bigalke, displays the new pendant designed by the K.C. Cornelius Jewelry Co.

One new event became an immediate hit—the Talent on Ice show, which took place at the Wayzata Ice Center. At the coronation ceremony that year D. W. Onan and Sons, Inc. formed a 34-piece employee chorus that sang as Queen Sharon Bigalke passed on her crown. The thirty-six-piece band of the Strategic Air Command from Omaha, Nebraska, also got into the act, performing at many festival events during the week and at the Coronation itself, held at the Minneapolis Auditorium.

Civic support for the festival remained strong as the decade drew to a close, with 787 businesses serving as members/corporate sponsors of the festival.

In 1959, a local jeweler, K.C. Cornelius Jewelry Co., created the exquisite official Queen of the Lakes pendant which was presented to the Aquatennial by the Minneapolis Jaycees. Queen Gail Nygaard was the first to wear the pendant in her official capacity at her coronation in 1959. The piece consisted of a heart-shaped aquamarine stone surrounded by thirty-one diamonds woven into a ribbon. The pendant was to be worn at all official functions and to be passed from Queen to Queen, though retiring Queens received a miniature copy. In addition to the stunning new pendant, Queen Gail introduced a new, floor-length, *peau de soie* robe designed by Charles Edwards, with Austrian rhinestones on the front ribbon bow. The robe was presented to Queen Sharon to be showcased at the coronation of the new Queen. Schlampp Furs completed the royal ensemble with a detachable Emba Jasmine mink cape which could also be worn separately as a stole. The robe was passed from Queen to Queen with the names embroidered inside, but each Queen got to keep her mink stole.

from Broadway. The canoe derby had been revived and the 1959 winners received a $13,000 cash and merchandise jackpot. That year's commodore, Randy Merriman, was a local boy who'd left Minneapolis to become a media star in New York as host of the nationally broadcast television show *The Big Payoff,* with former Miss America Bess Myerson as his co-host.

The 60s

Changes both large and small were in store as the Aquatennial entered its third decade. Some were brilliant innovations, some reflected the changing times, and others came about in response to past failures and successes.

In 1960, for the first time, academic scholarships were awarded to the Queen of the Lakes and Princesses by the Admirals Foundation. The Queen received $1,000 towards her education.

Also for the first time that year, the Aquatennial (along with the Bald Eagle Water Ski Club of White Bear Lake) hosted the National Water Ski Championships held at Lake of the Isles. More than 30,000 spectators attended.

The Music Festival of Aquatennial expanded to become a National Music Contest. Its repertoire included outstanding, "best of the best" young artists who excelled in instrumentals, organ, choral, pop singing, piano, vocal solo,

concert band, and accordion solos. The NW National Life Insurance Company sponsored music scholarships as well as trophies and other awards.

The ten days of festivities opened with two hundred fifty paratroopers from the 101st Airborne staging a parachute drop at the Anoka Airport.

Prior to that grand overture, teams of canoeists had once again been feverishly plying the Mississippi River between Grand Rapids and Minneapolis for more than a week. It was to be the last year of the marathon Paul Bunyan Canoe Derby, and it's fitting that famous canoe-racer and designer Gene Jensen and his partner won it. Jensen had already won the race three times—in 1948, 1949, and 1950. (Among other achievements, Jensen is credited with inventing the now-ubiquitous bent-shaft canoe paddle and the classic canoe shout, "Hut!")

The new Queen, Judy Mellin, was the last to be crowned at the Minneapolis Auditorium. An audience of 15,000 applauded as she was chosen from a bevy of worthy candidates.

A cadre of more than 2,500 civic-minded volunteers continued to coordinate the 210 events scheduled that year, which drew more than a million viewers and participants, including more than a hundred thousand who arrived from out-of-state solely to attend the Aquatennial.

The entertainment was top-notch throughout the festival, and a new event at Metropolitan Stadium, Music on Parade, brought an extraordinary line-up of performers together, including Mahalia Jackson, Woody Herman and his Thundering Herd, and the snappy jazz vocal trio Lambert, Hendricks, and Ross.

HI SKIPPER! MINNEAPOLIS 1962 AQUATENNIAL

Guess the Queen

You — yes you! — may win a new 1962 Pontiac Catalina convertible by correctly guessing the 1963 Aquatennia Queen of the Lakes. It's easy — just pick up an entry blank at any of the convenient Aquatennial ticket offices.

And remember, Aquatennial Skipper Pins give you special price advantages to key Aquatennial events.

In 1961, Hansord Pontiac provided a white Pontiac Bonneville convertible for the Queen's appearances throughout the year. The festival name and the Queen's name were painted in aqua-tinted script on both sides of the car for immediate recognition!

The *Minneapolis Star* newspaper featured photos of each Queen candidate as part of the "Guess the Queen" contest coordinated with the sale of Skipper Pins. The winner, announced at the Coronation Ball, received a Pontiac Catalina convertible. Two winners in the early 60's were Judy Havstad and Mrs. Harold Weidenhamer, Sr.

Jack Daly brought his then-wildly-popular daytime television show, *Queen for a Day*, to town for the entire

THE ROSE BOWL

The Minnesota Golden Gophers football team played in the Rose Bowl in 1961 and 1962, and Pam Albinson, the 1962 Aquatennial Queen, appeared in the Rose Bowl Parade that year. Here she delivers mail to Robin Tellor, Sandy Stephens, John Mulvena, Bob Sadek, coach Joe Salem, and Bob Frisee.

1961 festival. Day after day, local women told their sob stories to a national audience in hopes of being crowned Queen for a Day and receiving the cars and washing machines that accompanied the title.

Meanwhile, the short-lived TV show *The Blue Angels* heightened interest in the the death-defying U.S. Navy Flying Blue Angels air show that flew over the festival regularly, impressing viewers with their breathtaking close maneuvers.

It was so hot in 1961 that first aid stations were set up all along the Grande Day parade route to aid marchers—especially band members—who might otherwise succumb to dehydration during the four-mile-long parade.

Janelle Taylor remembers how proud her Granite Falls, Minnesota, Kilowatts Marching Band was to appear in the parade; but she also remembers how excruciatingly hot they all were. The band could afford only one set of uniforms—and they were wool! The Anoka Anoka-dettes Marching Band performed in the parade that year in outfits that included classy Bermuda shorts.

As luck would have it, in 1961 the Minneapolis Ciné Club filmed throughout the ten days of the festival, producing a twenty-eight-minute movie, *The Aquatennial Story*, with both sound and color. More than fifty years later, this remains the definitive film of early Aquatennial.

Half a million viewers enjoyed the Grande Day Parade that year, and three-quarters of a million lined the two-and-a-half-mile Torchlight Parade route. Sixty majestically decorated floats and thirty-five bands glittered and paraded down Nicollet Avenue. Sitting resplendent atop the Donaldson's Canopy, the Royal party waved to the passing parade participants.

Parade audiences went wild when the Indianhead Council Boy Scout Drum and Bugle Corp let loose with their thunderous sounds.

A new song, "Her Majesty The Queen," was written to honor the 1962 Queen of the Lakes and performed for the Coronation Ball by the Naval Band.

Murray Warmath's University of Minnesota Golden Gophers football team became the stuff of legend after playing in the Rose Bowl football games in both 1961 and 1962. Queens of the Lakes Judy Mellin (1961) and Pamela Jo Albinson (1962) were guests of honor at the Pasadena Tournament of Roses Parade during those years. Both Queens rode on exquisite flower-festooned floats representing the Aquatennial, the city of Minneapolis, and the University of Minnesota. Queen Judy rode on the Florist Telegraph Float accompanied by Tab Hunter. Queen Pam graced the very first City of Minneapolis float (opposite page) which was awarded the First Prize Presidential Award. Minnesotans flocked to Pasadena for the warm weather, the Tournament of Roses festivities...and the football.

Left: The Dayton's float during the 1961 Grande Parade. Above: Queen Connie Haenny (1963) appeared on the Steve Allen Show.

The Aquatennial got off to a festive start on opening night in 1962 when nine Fairchild transport planes—Flying Boxcars—dropped a hundred thousand balloons on the city of Minneapolis. Most of the balloons were empty, but a few of them contained $5,000 in prizes, all of which were up for grabs.

The National Music Festival winners performed at the Queen's coronation that year, and the Minneapolis Ciné Club's film, *The Aquatennial Story*, had its premiere. The 1960 Aquatennial Queen, Gail Nygaard, appeared as one of the Aqua Dears in the Follies.

The famed Cypress Gardens Water Show of Orlando, Florida, gave exciting performances.

Don McNeill was delighted to bring his homespun network "Breakfast Club" back to town. And the King and Queen from Brazil's Carnival dazzled parade-goers with their stunning historic costume ensembles covered with beads, glitter, and sparkly splendor (opposite page).

In 1963, for the first time, every Queen candidate was required to ride on her community float or a business float rather than in a convertible. Parade organizers felt there were too many vehicles in the parades, and more visual excitement was needed. Also that year, twenty past Queens formed an alumni group, the Past Queens Organization; and the Board of Directors

Aquatennial attractions during the mid-1960s ranged from turtle races (above) and aquatic daring do (top) to stunning royal guests from the Carnival in Rio (left).

created the new position of General Festival Chairman. The first to serve in this capacity was Paul Mans. KSTP–TV televised both Aquatennial parades in color for the first time, and Queen Pam Albinson appeared with Jim Hutton as parade narrators for the Grande Day Parade.

That year Queen Connie Haenny was accompanied on her Florist Telegraph float by Martin Milner, star of the TV show *Route 66*, and during Milner's visit the episode, "Where Are the Sounds of Celli Brahms?" was filmed in Minneapolis. It aired on October 18, 1963.

In 1964 the Aquatennial celebrated its silver anniversary. A twenty-five-layer cake weighing several hundred pounds was baked for the occasion. It was twelve feet high with a twelve-foot-square base. Many of the original founders were on hand at the celebratory party held in the Leamington Hotel's Hall of States. (The Leamington had served for many years as the Aquatennial headquarters during festival time.)

But that same year's festival turned out to be the last to host the Aqua Follies at Theodore Wirth Lake. Although the rise of television had undercut the appeal of such spectacles somewhat, the event was still popular. But after a quarter-century of use and exposure to the elements, the stage, bleachers, and diving area were in serious need of repairs, and the Aquatennial Board did not deem it fiscally prudent to do the work.

The featured attraction for the silver anniversary celebration was Aqua City, an ensemble of striped canvas pavilions erected at the north end of Nicollet Avenue, near the finishing point of the Aquatennial parades. Local international groups danced in native costume, as did

Queen of the Lakes Mary Margaret Shultz lights a candle on a facsimile of the huge silver anniversary cake, surrounded by the Vice Commodore division. From left to right: Nick Sachs (Parades), Vern Gust (Hospitality), Don Krez (Sports and Lakes), Robert Grandquist (Chairman), Bob Benham (Music and Parks), Don Fox (Queens), and Lou Hough (Special Events).

representatives of several Minnesota Indian tribes. An elaborate system of fountains was put in place offering "light shows" of sparkling water both day and night. Local restaurants served food from booths, and theatrical groups put on plays at Aqua City's central stage. The entire Aqua City was illuminated at night by gaslight.

Another new event for 1964 was Organ Fantasy. Eddie Dunstedter, famed keyboard artist on the fabulous

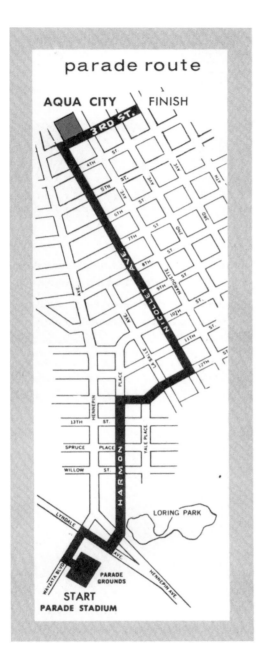

parade route

AQUA CITY   FINISH

LORING PARK

START
PARADE STADIUM

Wurlitzer, was joined at Parade Stadium by two other musicians—Shay Torrent and Axel Alexander—to play three electronically intertwined Hammond organs simultaneously. Nearly $20,000 of speaker equipment was employed to ensure perfect sound for the concert.

In 1965, Aquatennial organizers brought in an Aqua Holiday Show to replace the Aqua Follies at Wirth Lake, featuring the Aqua-Maids precision water ballet troupe. The singing duo of Nelson Eddy and Gale Sherwood were also part of the new show, as was famed Acapulco cliff diver Raul Gracia, who dove into the pool from a platform one hundred feet above the water.

The festival theme that year was "Our Neighbors to the South," and Dayton's transformed its eighth floor auditorium into a Mexican village square where the Mexican State Ballet Folklorico troupe performed and Mexican artisans demonstrated various skills daily.

Workers and visitors to downtown Minneapolis were treated to daily carillon performances; Verdin, the famous Dutch bell manufacturer, had brought a set of 20 cast bronze bells to town weighing from 20 to 583 pounds; it was their first formal appearance in the United States. On an entirely different note, the Village Stompers, a Dixieland band, was featured

Above: In 1965, some of the nation's top road-racing drivers competed at speeds approaching 150 m.p.h at the Land-O-Lakes Sports Car Classic.

Left: A map showing the parade route and the location of Aqua City.

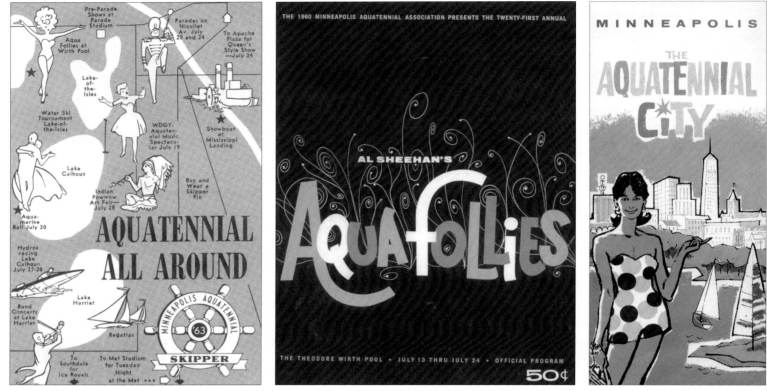

These three graphics from the early-to-mid 1960s reflect the competing claims of tradition and innovation as Aquatennial promoters worked to maintain interest in their programs and activities.

daily at shows sponsored by the Southdale Merchants Association.

When Mary Sue Anderson was chosen Queen of the Lakes in 1965, she became the third to hail from Gustavus Adolphus College in St. Peter. Ruth Tolman (1947) and Lee Jaenson (1949) had also attended the college.

The festival had a "three-peat" of a different sort the following year, when Hubert Humphrey served as Grand Marshall. Humphrey's first appearance in that capacity had been in 1945, when he was Mayor of Minneapolis. Four years later he returned to the parade as a U.S. Senator. By 1966 Humphrey had been elected Vice President of the United States. (Incidentally, Humphrey was the third Vice President to serve as Grand Marshall. Richard Nixon and Alben Barkley had preceded him.)

Times had changed radically since 1945, and so had styles and interests. New buildings were going up downtown, but the suburbs were enjoying most of the fruits of growth. Meanwhile, the arrival of rock-and-roll had revolutionized the entertainment industry.

In 1966 Aquatennial organizers decided to look to the past, emphasizing America's historical traditions. Six blocks of Nicollet Avenue strove to recreate or exemplify six different periods of American history: The Old West, the Colonial South, the Gay Nineties, the Roaring Twenties, Exotic America, and contemporary life—an era dubbed "the Soaring Sixties." Each block had its own unique sights and sounds ranging from country western music to barbershop quartets and devil-may-care flappers. Six parade divisions were created to represent the six historic periods, each with its own equestrian unit, creative theme float, and costumed marching band.

Dayton's created an authentic Hawaiian village on its eighth floor. And since the Aqua Follies were kaput, the stage at Theodore Wirth Lake was given over to a new "Aqua Pops" program that presented *The Sound of Music* with Dorothy Collins, America's "singing sweetheart," and *The Music Man* starring Bert Parks, the perennial host of Miss America pageants. Unfortunately, these new productions were not deemed a success—perhaps because film versions of both musicals had recently enjoyed outstanding runs in movie theaters.

The Queen of the Lakes that year, Linda Kleinert, was thrilled to be presented with a diamond tiara for her royal appearances by Kirchner's Kaynar Diamonds. The piece consists of 218 diamonds with a 3.2 marquise cut on the top of the design. It totaled 56.67 karats and was valued at $45,000. After the festival the diamonds were removed and fashioned into engagement rings (see photo on page 79).

Above: The glass-sheathed First National Bank building, completed in 1960, was the first major post-war skyscraper to be erected in Minneapolis. Its plaza played host to many Aquatennial events.

The year 1967 saw the Aquatennial organizers finally get into the youth scene in a big way. Sonny and Cher agreed to perform at an Aquatennial event at the Minneapolis Convention Hall on July 14, but Cher suffered a miscarriage three days before the show, and Sonny only reluctantly agreed to appear, singing duets with a string of local female vocalists who had hastily auditioned for the rare opportunity.

A more robust three-day show at the Minneapolis Auditorium, labelled Happening '67, featured

Left: A new perspective was added to parade-watching in the 1960s—the skyways.
Right: A poster advertising the Aquatennial-sponsored psychedelic Happening '67

acid-rock bands Jefferson Airplane ("White Rabbit") and the Electric Prunes ("I had too Much to Dream Last Night"); alt-rock band Buffalo Springfield, which included Stephen Stills (Neil Young had recently departed); and Shadows of Night, a now-largely-forgotten band that had recently recorded the hit single "Gloria," which was easy to play and was then being "covered" by garage bands throughout the United States. Reporter Molly Ivins, a *Tribune* staff writer at the time, observed after the show: "If most of the kids were hippies, then they were too young to grow beards."

Queen of the Lakes Karen Erlandson was the last to wear the official 1948 Coronation Crown. Her new robe, which she first wore at the Tournament of Roses Parade in Pasadena, was designed by Jacques Heim of Paris, France. Made of deep blue *aleoutienne* silk lined with matching *faille*, the robe was worn with the traditional white mink stole. It was commissioned by Montgomery Ward, and replaced the blue satin robe introduced in 1959.

In 1967, Aqua Spectacular, a two-hour stage and water show from Miami, Florida, made its inaugural appearance at the new Minneapolis Auditorium, making use of two large portable pools. The Aqua Maids were the precision swimmers. And Barney Cipriani, five times world professional diving champion thrilled everyone with his ninety-foot dive into seven feet of water ringed with flames from a perch suspended from the auditorium ceiling.

That same year, Dayton's eighth floor auditorium featured Safari Across Africa, with African singers, dancers, musicians, and craftsmen. N. Ade Martins, the Nigerian Ambassador to the U.S., opened the event. Jim Lange, a Native Minnesotan and host of the ABC-TV show *The Dating Game*, was another special Aqua guest. The two winners from his July 4 show were invited to ride in the Grande Day Parade.

But 1967 has since become known as The Long Hot Summer, due to riots that erupted throughout

Above: The Kirchner's Kaynar Diamonds tiara.

Right: The new Jacques Heim robe.

Below: Queen candidates from around the state enjoy a relaxing cruise on Lake Minnetonka to calm their nerves before the coronation ceremony.

Gail Nygaard

Judy Mellin

Pam Albinson

Connie Haenny

Mary Schultz

Mary Sue Anderson

Linda Kleinert

Karen Erlandson

Karen Hegener

Janet Johnson

The 60s

79

Left: 1953 Junior Queen Nancy Piazza eating spaghetti at her dad's restaurant, Cafe di Napoli.

Above: Nancy with Marguerite Piazza, Metropolitan Opera star

JUNIOR QUEEN

My relationship with the Minneapolis Aquatennial started in 1953, when I was five. I remember my mother bringing me downtown to my dad's restaurant, Cafe di Napoli, where I met my godmother, who happened to be the cashier. She told me that if I won the Junior Queen contest, she would buy me the billfold she'd seen me eyeing at Dayton's. I took up the challenge.

I remember walking with my mom over to the Pick-Nicollet Hotel where the contest was being held. There, I was escorted to a room where other little girls were anxiously waiting for their turn to talk to the judges. This seemed easy for me, as I always enjoyed talking with grown-ups.

"What does your dad do?" I was asked. I answered, "My dad makes spaghetti," and watched as the judges began to laugh! *This is fun*, I thought, and went back to sit down.

I won the contest, and this feeling of fun and laughter lasted with me all the way through my year as Junior Queen. What captured my imagination especially were the bright lights of the floats and the sparkling decorations; the smells coming from the cars pulling the floats; the smell of the street vendors and shouts of the enthusiastic crowds. It was all like a fairy tale. I was on a throne with my princesses around me. (There was no

Junior Commodore then.) Everyone would wave at us, and I eagerly waved back. Some of the Princesses would cry because they were afraid—but not me. I felt this was the best party ever. Junior Queens were included in most of the Aquatennial events for that year, including parades, luncheons, opportunities to model fancy dresses, and the glamorous crowning of the new Queen of the Lakes at Theodore Wirth Aqua Follies pool.

All of this excitement would be repeated fourteen years later, in 1967, when I won the crown of Miss Golden Valley, and I found myself a part of Aquatennial once again. My parade float was a gondola just like the ones in Venice. How appropriate to have an Italian girl on an Italian float! Once again, the lights, sounds, smells, and friendly crowds flooded back. Minneapolis was so alive. I was amazed at how well organized it all was. But, I do remember a racial disturbance towards the end of the parade. Immediately the candidate floats were directed to a different street where we rapidly disembarked for a quick return to our hotels.

As Queen candidates, we were often being watched by the judges. I noticed that some of the girls were less friendly when the judges weren't around. I became such good friends with my roommate, Miss Granite Falls, that I was even in her wedding. On the final day of interviews I was told if I became the Queen I would have to drop out of college for one year. For me that was not possible, and I was happy with my decision. Returning to our hotel after the coronation, I discovered that my father had sent over pizza for us all. Perfect! Italian pizza for an Italian Queen and her new found friends.

– Nancy Piazza, 2014

the United States, including Minneapolis. Police with helmets and riot gear offered a sobering contrast to the Aquatennial's often light-hearted festivities, and tensions were high. There was rioting, property loss due to fire, and charges of police brutality after the Torchlight Parade.

In fact, in 1968 there was talk of canceling the Torchlight Parade. Organizers decided instead to encourage

Upper left: The Sabathani Drum and Bugle Corps had been popular among festival-goers for years.

Upper right: At the AquaTeen Road Rally.

Above: The St. Louis Park Parkettes offered a line dance clinic.

African Americans to play a more active role in the 1968 festival. One initiative, the Citizen's Patrol, made up of both blacks and whites, helped with crowd control during the parades and the Aretha Franklin concert.

The theme that year was Northern Seas, and festival organizers imported fifteen hundred pounds of frozen haddock from Norway to serve at The World's Largest Fish Fry on the shores of Lake Calhoun. More than five thousand people attended. At another event, five outstanding chefs from Scandinavia demonstrated the intricacies of preparing Danish, Finnish, Norwegian, and Swedish cuisine.

During International Children's Day that year, a children's film festival was held, and all children were encouraged to wear costumes from foreign lands. And a touring exhibition, Spotlight on Germany, featured a display of more than five thousand industrial and consumer goods in the Exhibition Hall of the Minneapolis Auditorium. Meanwhile, six rare Westphalian horses pulled floats in the parade, impressing the crowds with their grace and splendor.

Nicollet Mall, which had been under construction for two years, was finally opened in 1968, in time to play host to many Aquatennial events. The mall was the first "transit mall" to be installed in the United States, and it soon inspired similar renovations in Portland, Denver, and other cities.

In 1969, as the Aquatennial completed its third decade, some traditions remained strong, others had faded, and new activities were continually being offered. That year a line-dancing competition was added, and a "highly amplified" Beach Party was held at Lake Calhoun.

Above: An art fair was held on the newly pedestrianized Nicollet Mall.
Below: Square dancing at the First National Bank Plaza.

From the very first, parades have been among the most popular Aquatennial events. There have traditionally been two blockbuster parades, the Torchlight Parade and the Grande Day Parade. All sorts of groups have participated, from high school marching bands to drum and bugle corps, cheerleaders twirling batons, Aqua Jesters, and floats of every shape and size. Local businesses and organizations take pride in sponsoring the creation and maintenance of floats for these events and many of them are works of art in their own right.

Municipalities throughout the state also bring floats to Aquatennial events to showcase their cities and their candidates for Queen of the Lakes.

For decades, the Shriners brought additional razzle dazzle to parades with their raucous revelry. The Zurah Temple Band, Changers, Chief of Staff, Colors and Color Guard, Drum Corps, Legion of Honor, Motorcycles, Mini-cars, Horse Patrol and other colorfully coordinated groups lit up the parade and excited the crowds.

Clockwise from upper left: Dayton's Queen candidate on Dayton's float; A Showboat float from New Orleans; The Shriners marching band; A Theatre of Seasons float sponsored by Donaldsons.

AQUATENNIAL PARADES

Ken Hafften

The first Aquatennial Grande Day Parade in 1940 was a parade of significant proportions including eighty-six floats, fifty bands/drum corps, and more than fifteen thousand marchers in Aquatennial uniforms. Forty city blocks were required for the parade assembly. Nicollet Avenue was lined with bleachers to accommodate ten to fifteen thousand spectators, and more than 200,000 more viewed the parade from curbside, office windows, hanging from street lights, or wherever they could find a spot.

Early parades began in downtown Minneapolis and ended at the Parade grounds. Later parades began at the Parade grounds and ended in downtown Minneapolis. A stadium built at the Parade grounds in 1951, primarily for football games, made it possible to have reserved seating at the beginning of the parades. The parades in the late 1980s began in Northeast Minneapolis, crossed the Mississippi River on the Third Avenue Bridge, and ended downtown. The present Torchlight Parade begins at the Dunwoody area and proceeds down Hennepin Avenue.

All large parades have three logistical areas: assembly, route, and dispersal. In the assembly area, the units are segregated in a separate location by unit type in the order that the particular unit will enter the parade. At the "mixing valve," these stands come together and are sent off in the proper order. Close to one hundred volunteers are required to review and approve applications for the Aquatennial parades and then to plan and produce them. At every block along the parade route, there is a route volunteer with an assigned radio operator to ensure that the parade moves smoothly. Health care personnel are strategically stationed to assist parade participants who might need them. This is especially important on hot and humid parade days when heat exhaustion is a constant threat. Also stationed along the route are tow trucks ready to help floats and other motorized units that became disabled.

As the times have changed, Aquatennial parades have also changed. The early parades were both massive in participation as well as number of spectators. Throughout the 1940s, most of the floats were sponsored by Minneapolis businesses; it wasn't until the 1950s that community festivals began sponsoring the floats that today make up the bulk of the Torchlight Parade. Until recently, the parade floats were judged in the assembly area, vying for several awards, with Minneapolis floats having an edge due to the presence of three prominent local float builders: Brede, Shumakers, and Vaughn Displays. The character of those riding on floats has also changed—from attractive young women in swim suits to talented young women in gowns, usually representing their local communities.

The bands have also changed over time. In the early years they were primarily military and community bands with a few high school bands intermixed. The most in-

This float from a 1949 parade celebrates Minnesota agriculture, milling, and industry.

Everybody loves a parade!

tense high school band competition in the early 1940s, but it was always the Ames Elk Lodge Drum and Bugle Corps that "stole the show." The most well-known community band today is the Robbinsdale City Band, which has appeared in every Aquatennial parade.

During the 1980s and 1990s, a significant effort was put forth to differentiate the Grande Day Parade from the Torchlight Parade. The Grande Day Parade was organized and marketed as a family parade and combined with other family events both before and after the parade. The Torchlight Parade was designed to be the spectacular signature event. The Saturday Grande Day Parade was discontinued after 2004 due to lack of interest, but the Torchlight Parade remains popular.

Ken Hafften has been a parade volunteer (42 years), Parade Vice Commodore (1988), three term Vice Commodore (1988-1990), GFC (1991), and Captain (1995).

THE LIFE OF A "FLOATER"

STEVE SHUMAKER

What was it like building and driving parade floats? For that matter, what was it like growing up around them?

When I was a youngster, Dad's (Gordy Shumaker) shop was right behind our house. For the first few years of my life, I was in that world every day. All the floats, sets and Christmas decorations were my "normal."

I attended many Aquatennial parades throughout my childhood, and had a unique perspective. My sisters, Lori and Debi, rode quite a few floats during those years, including one for Grain Belt Breweries that carried a live tiger in a cage! That was my first up-close encounter with a tiger—but far from my last.

I finally "got" to work on floats as an employee of Dad's business, Gordon Displays, the summer I turned thirteen. While my junior high classmates were attending summer camp, playing Little League, or working paper routes, I was helping build parade floats along with my brothers, Greg and Todd, as well as my sisters.

To build a float requires a multitude of talented people, or a multitude of talents among a few people. It begins with the designer, who lets his or her imagination flow, coming up with a sketch of what the finished float will look like. The dimensions of the sketch are based on real-world scale of how the floats will be built. The welders and carpenters take over, preparing and building the float bed as needed. The mechanic works on the drive-train and power generators that will move

Clockwise from upper left: Snyder's float; a "float" that actually floated during the inaugural Aquatennial in 1940; a Twinkle, Twinkle float; and Dayton's Banana float.

the float and light it for the Torchlight Parade. The sculptor makes the props, and the animation specialist makes them move. The electrician puts on the flood, border, and specialty lights, and wires the animation. The artists paint the props and decorate the float. The sign painter puts on the logos and names. The sound tech provides music and sound effects. Come parade day, the navigators and drivers then move the floats to the line-up area, through the parade, and back to the shop.

In Dad's shop, the artist who designed the float would often build the props, decorate the float, paint the signs (all of our signs were hand-painted), and then drive the float in the parade. The mechanic, electrician, animation, and sound technician were often the same person, and he sometimes drove the float, too. Everyone worked almost every job. Even when it came to sweeping up afterwards, everybody, including Gordy, leant a hand.

If there was one constant at the shop, it was that every project, every day, would be different from the last. No design would ever be repeated. Clients would have an entirely new float each and every year. The show would be continually changed and upgraded. Many clients of Gordon Displays put floats in the Aquatennial for several decades, including Hamm's, Grain Belt, Northwestern Bell (now Quest), Ford, Economics Laboratories (now Ecolab), Whirlpool, Hilex, and Dayton's, which consistently sponsored the most creative float, year after year.

As parade day approached, work days got longer, and weekends increasingly rare. Being a proud World

Queen of the Lakes Maureen Wagner (1971) with her intrepid driver

War II Navy veteran, Gordy always closed the shop on Memorial Day and the Fourth of July. Everyone welcomed the break, but it wasn't unheard of to find that one or two employees had come in to work on a project in solitude.

With July fifth came the big push, as only a few weeks remained to finish the floats before the Grand Day Parade. That meant no days off, and more than a few twelve-, fourteen-, and even sixteen-hour days. Some days just spilled into others. Life outside the shop didn't exist. Food was brought in.

"We were cleaning up, ready to go home," recalled artist Bob Edgett. "Then in walks Gordy with bags of White Castle hamburgers. I knew we were there for the night."

Even exhausted, some people kept at the job. "This one fella was so tired, he fell asleep while working on his project" said Shirley Shumaker. "He had been working on a chicken-wire form, and just slept right there, his nose hanging in the chicken-wire."

The parade itself brought a new set of challenges. Our crews always rose to the occasion. The floats endured a bit of shaking on the way to the parade, and loose items had to be reattached in the line-up area. Some pieces were intentionally left off until just before the parade. Mechanics needed a final check before the floats moved out, and fuel needed to be topped off. When dealing with running more than a dozen big floats in the parade, it was inevitable that something would be forgotten. There would be a mad rush to correct the problem, even as the float was heading into Parade Stadium.

The larger and more elaborate the float, the more difficult it was to handle. The crews relished the challenge, and many wanted to drive the bigger floats. The most experienced drivers typically drove the bigger floats, but on occasion, someone had worked so hard on a particular float that it seemed only proper that he should get to drive it. One driver even offered to work the parade for free—if he could drive the float of his choice. He liked driving the "open" jeeps and he loved the Shakopee Mdewakanton Sioux Community float sponsored by Mystic Lake Casino. That float became "his" for several seasons.

For ten years I drove floats carrying the Queen of the Lakes and the Princesses in a dozen big parades each season. Naturally, my choice for the Aquatennial parades would be to drive that particular float, which was often one of the biggest we made. The last Queen I drove on a regular basis was Sandy Polesky, accompanied by Princesses Ann Minks and Jody Peterson. Their big finale was the Aquatennial parades, and the float that year had them sitting in very high seats (not my idea) nearly six feet above the float's deck and nine feet above the street. I had to lift each of them by the waist and put them in their seats. Luckily, I was young and strong after many summers of wrestling lumber and steel around, and they were light!

The following year, I may have squeezed Queen Jennifer Tolrud too hard and bruised her ribs while putting her in that high seat. Sorry!

The Shakopee Mdewakanton Sioux Community float

Above: Roy Wilhite and a Hamm's Bear with chipmunks
Below: The workshop ca 1990

I hope I'm not giving you the impression that the float driver's life is all glamour, hanging out with beautiful, outgoing young women; in truth, it's mostly work. There are several floats to prep for the parade, and time is always at a premium. There is always something to set up or a problem to fix. Just getting the floats into their proper places in the line-up can be a major chore, gobbling up lots of time.

Parades usually go off without a hitch, but it's the surprises that stand out. One year, we were a bit late in getting to the parade. The Queen of the Lakes float was last in line, but a couple of snags on the streets forced us to park it at the front of the line-up, just around the corner. We had plenty of time to prep everything for the parade—or so we thought. One of the parade directors, Angus Dow, kept coming over, repeatedly asking if we'd be ready to go, as the parade was about to start. I replied that there was plenty of time, because we were last in the parade. He looked at me and said, *"No you're not. You're first!"* I was shocked! I asked to see the order-of-march sheet, and sure enough, we were first—but nobody had told us! The float's regular crew was a couple of blocks down the street, prepping other floats. I sent one of the other guys running down to get them.

In the meantime, the truck used to transport the float to the parade was still parked in front of it, and needed to be moved around behind it, out of the way. The Minneapolis Police Band had lined up next to the float, blocking access. The driver couldn't get them to move. I told him to get in the truck, and move at my signal. I jumped into the back, and got the band's attention. I explained the situation (just shortening it to an emergency) and politely asked them to briefly step aside. One of the members said, *"We're not allowed to break rank!"* which is what I expected. I replied, *"Well then you're gonna get run over."* I signaled my driver to go. They moved. I thanked them for their understanding and cooperation. The Queen and Princesses arrived, and I put them into their lofty seats. The crew showed up, we started the float, without a moment to spare: it was time to go!

The float riders don't usually show up until the parade is about to start (often, they have their own appearance schedules to meet), and the driver has little time to get them situated before the parade directors frantically implore them to get going. Once the float starts moving, it's all business. It takes all the driver's attention and skill to keep the float moving straight and in pace with the units in front of it. Corners can be a challenge for the big floats, as well as big crowds spilling into the streets.

The drivers had to keep an eye not only on the street, but on how their vehicle is running—breakdowns happen, even with brand-new equipment—how the generator is running, that the lights and animation is working properly, and making sure any music and/or intercom systems are working properly throughout the parade. Most importantly, the driver is responsible for the safety of those who are riding the float. They come first.

The sheer physical challenge of driving a big float was often compounded by the heat and humidity of late July. The temperatures inside a covered float could rise to 120 degrees or more. Fans provided some relief, but nothing felt as good as the relief of getting out of those floats at the end of the parade—even when the temperatures were in the high 80s!

As our floats reached the dispersal area, the riders got off and headed to their next event, and the floats were prepped for the trip home. We had anywhere between one to two dozen floats to convoy home in any given Aquatennial. After the Torchlight Parade, the lights on all the floats would be left on for the trip home. Imagine the sight of all those floats moving down the street en masse, all lit up! It was as thrilling as the parade itself.

It could take an hour to get all the floats back to the shop, even though it was normally a ten- to fifteen-minute drive. It would take a couple more hours to get everything put away properly. It was often past midnight before the doors were closed and everybody could go home. Even so, some would linger, telling stories of their experiences in the parade. The cheers and applause of the crowds were a common theme of discussion.

The day after the Torchlight Parade, the shop is a quiet, lonely place. All the people who were called in to help are gone. After weeks of frenzied activity, we now have extra time on our hands. We don't quite know what to do with our evenings and weekends. But in less than a week, many of the big floats would be making an appearance in Northeast Minneapolis's Central Avenue parade. Our float will carry the new Queen of the Lakes into another new season.

Steve Shumaker is a free-lance artist living in Arden Hills. He specializes in parade floats and Halloween Haunts.

Fantasies on Parade

K. Marie O'Brien

A designer's sketch for a Grain Belt mermaid float

You may have some vivid memories of Aquatennial parades, perhaps from years ago when you were a child, or more recently, when you took your children or grandchildren to see one. Take a minute to remember it. Close your eyes and put yourself back on the street. What do you see? What do you smell? What sounds do you hear? Are you hot? Wet? Are you eating ice cream or cotton candy? Is it daylight or nighttime?

Chances are that the passing floats play a significant role in those memories. Though many things contribute to making a parade successful, floats seem to hold the most allure. If you've ever wondered about those floats—where they come from, how they're designed and built, what materials are used in building them, who builds and drives them, how they get to the parade, and even what happens to them after the last unit passes by you on the street—you'll find the answers in this article.

Every float begins with a design concept and an artist's rendering. Once that's completed, potential sponsors have an opportunity to view the designs. Some designs fit into specific categories that match the parade theme; others fit into the theme the sponsor wants to portray.

The most popular and best loved, as well as the most-well remembered floats, are often the ones that tell a story, conjure up fantastical voyages, or mimic historical venues. Any float with a humorous touch is also likely to please the crowds.

Floats are essentially grand theater; those who design and construct them utilize many of the same techniques and face many of the same challenges that theater producers do. They must present things in "bigger than life" format. Backdrops, color, costumes, and lighting all serve to enhance the appeal.

Floats have always made use of the latest technologies, and with the advent of computers, fiber optic lighting, and hydraulics, designers have been able to push the envelope even further in recent years. But floats were already popular in ancient times. In Egypt, the Nile provided the perfect vehicle to transport the floats—which were also barges—and their riders.

One of the premiere float designers and builders for nearly sixty years—from the mid-1930s until the 1990s—was Gordon Shumaker (1915–2000). When the Aquatennial began in 1940, Shumaker was working in the display department of Snyder's Drug Stores, having started there in the mid-1930s. In 1937, he built his first float for Snyder's, to appear in the newly revived St. Paul Winter Carnival.

When America entered World War II in 1941, Shumaker joined the Navy. His artistic background earned him a job running the paint locker on board the battleship *USS Texas*. After the war, he returned to Snyder's display department, but he was soon hired away by the Winter Carnival organizers to build floats for them. He and his Navy buddy Don Lehan founded Don Displays in 1946 and formally incorporated the business two years later. Over the years, the company also did business as Gor-Don Displays, Gordon Displays and finally, Famous Floats.

Float designs in the early years were relatively simple, with many military-themed ones that saluted veterans, as well as corporate floats featuring company logos and products. In time those simple designs gave way to more fanciful ones based on fables and fairy tales. One of Shumaker's favorites from that early period was a Cinderella float where the big mice "pulling" a carriage would flip over and become horses.

From the late 1940s to the early1970s, designs became ever more intricate and creative, attracting the kind of attention that corporate sponsors were hungry for. Even small towns began to commission floats that were adventurous and unique.

The Grain Belt Trojan horse float

In the 1960s, Aquatennial themes began to take on an international flavor, and float designers were happy to exploit exotic locales such as India, Asia, Mexico, Greece, and the Middle East.

For example, in 1973 Grain Belt Brewery sponsored a Trojan horse float for the Aquatennial's Grande Parade. This impressive entry measured 50 feet long, 14 feet wide, and more than 16 feet tall. The horse's head was designed to duck as the float passed under bridges, skyways, and street lights. The job of lowering the

Dayton's Song of India float and the elephants leading it

thirteen when he worked on the float in his father's firm. "Diamond dust is ground glass, and we all had cuts on our feet from the glass getting into our shoes."

Though the float was actually powered by a jeep concealed within it, twenty slaves were supposed to "pull" ropes to simulate the ancient means of locomotion. Unfortunately, when parade day came, only two of the volunteer slaves showed up. Gordon Shumaker recruited other volunteers from the audience to participate, as well as his sons, Steve and Greg. Some went shirtless, while others wore white T-shirts and blue jeans. In the end, the recruitment effort was so successful that more rope was added to accomodate everyone.

"At some points during the parade," says Steve Shumaker, "fantasy turned into reality. The driver told us later that he occasionally disengaged the clutch, so we actually *were* pulling the float."

While many float occupants are "royalty," and most are human, there were many times over the years when nonhumans also appeared, including sled dogs, sheep, a tiger, Shetland ponies, and black bears. If the animals weren't actually *on* the floats, they accompanied it, either leading or surrounding it in some way.

Elephants served this purpose with a Dayton's float in 1957 called The Song of India. It had a Taj Mahal-type building on the back, its onion-shaped domes sheathed

head fell to Gordy's son Todd and his cousin Tim.

Like the Trojan horse described in *The Illiad*, the Grain Belt float was built of wood, but unlike the ancient one, the Aquatennial float was painted white and covered with diamond dust.

"Diamond dust is not a pleasant or healthy material to work with," says Steve Shumaker, who was only in real 18-karat gold leaf! The deck of the float was covered with Persian rugs for which Dayton's was famous. The float's big attraction though, was the three live, Indian elephants leading it; each painted a different pastel color—pink, orange, and yellow. The owner walked alongside the elephants, while Shumaker's wife, Shirley, her sister Betty, and a Dayton's employee rode on top.

The elephants were kept at the float shop for three weeks prior to the parades. Shumaker would feed them loaves of bread, and the elephants liked them so much they sometimes grabbed and swallowed them whole—wrapper and all.

"Dad would yell at them to wait," says Steve Shumaker, Gordon's son, "but they never would."

The elephants were also used to move the floats in and out of the shop, which was sometimes risky. As Steve recalls, they knew only one speed—fast. "Luckily, they didn't do much damage."

The elephants would also get a chance to cool off in Lake Calhoun. As soon as they smelled the water there was no stopping them. They had a lot of fun at the beach, and they drew quite a crowd.

Of the hundreds of floats built by the Shumaker firm, the ones sponsored by Dayton's were often the most

The "A Century of Fashion" float

memorable, for builders and the audiences alike. These floats were always elaborate and groundbreaking—the Song of India being one example among many.

Another innovative design was the Dayton's float built in 1956 to celebrate the City of Minneapolis's Centennial. The float was *167 feet long*! One jeep pulled ten trailers, with each trailer depicting a decade in the history of local fashion. The feat of building a float this long is extraordinary, and only in recent years has a float of this length been built again, and that was for the Tournament of Roses Parade in Pasadena, California.

Though a lot of effort and energy go into designing and building a float, for the most part they are short-term objects. Many floats are built for just two big parades, or a couple of large ones and a few smaller community ones. Once these events are over, the floats are torn down. However, the parts of many floats are recycled, sometimes more than once. A float trailer can last many years.

Weeks before parade day, the parade route must be driven and studied. The height of all bridges and overhangs must be measured, the angles of all turns noted and the width of the streets recorded. The route to and from the parade needs the same attention.

Weather can also be an issue. The dates for the

It's easy to overlook the drivers in these photos, due to the allure of the "cargo." In the lower photo, taken in 1979, Steve Shumaker is driving the float of Queen Becky Rear.

one parade, though it was not until 2002 that a parade was cancelled due to inclement weather.

Once a parade is over, the task remains of getting the floats back to the shop. They're usually assembled and driven in a caravan, but things don't always go so smoothly.

"One year, after a Torchlight Parade," Steve Shumaker recalls, "we had to drive around downtown Minneapolis looking for a float because the crew for that one had been directed by the sponsor's representative to turn down a different street for a volunteer party. Our crewman asked the sponsor if *I* knew about the diversion. 'Oh, I'm sure he does,' came the answer. Well, no. I didn't.

"The float was a large one that required a pick-up truck for locomotion. Plus, the steering mechanism was on the fritz. We had no idea where it was and finally left without it. We took the other floats back to the shop and put them away, then went back downtown to find our lost sheep, which had been parked down the block and around the corner on an empty side street."

Though new sources of personal entertainment abound in the twenty-first century, parade floats continue to evolve, too, and still have much to contribute.

"I've developed some of my most creative designs in just the past five years or so," says Shumaker. "I have drawers full of new sketches or modified sketches from old designs that were never produced. In some cases, a design that I wasn't sure how to produce, or that was likely to be too expensive, has now become feasible, due to advances in materials and technology.

Aquatennial were selected on the basis of advice from local meteorologists, who identified that week as statistically the driest of the summer. But it also tends to be among the hottest weeks, and thunderstorms are an ever-present possibility. Rain has fallen on more than

And I'm coming up with ideas that nobody has done anywhere before."

The Aquatennial parades and the floats that grace them are a part of Minneapolis's unique social heritage. Yet we seldom stop to ask ourselves: Who made that? How did that get put together? Where's the driver?

Today's floats may seem like an anacronism to some, yet there is no better way for a community to express its values, traditions, and shared commitment to "the good life."

K. Marie O'Brien is a writer and artist living in Arden Hills, Minnesota. She began working in the Shumaker float business in 1986. The fact that her husband is the Steve Shumaker profiled in this article helps, too.

As the Aquatennial entered its fourth decade, more than 2,500 volunteers continued to bring the festival to life with their enthusiastic commitment to individual events and also to the community. The theme for 1970, Seas of the Orient, brought hundreds of members of the Thai, Korean, Chinese, Japanese, Taiwanese, and Filipino communities together. They spent many hours organizing events and raising money to finance their parade floats and other attractions based on their cultures. One such contribution was the Chinese Arch, the design and color of which blended beautifully into the cityscape. The arch became an instant downtown landmark, and when the decision was made to remove it to the International Center at the State Fairgrounds, it created quite a stir.

In 1971, the first annual Aquatennial Masters Golf Tournament was hosted by Chi Chi Rodriguez. That was also the year the perennially popular Milk Carton Boat Races were first held on Lake Calhoun. The event had been conceived a year earlier by local advertising agency Campbell-Mithun and the American Dairy Association. The two organizations were brainstorming for a new event that would focus on water but also involve milk somehow, with the idea in mind of getting teens to drink more of it. One of the attendees mentioned that an empty half-gallon milk carton can keep up to four pounds afloat. The end result was the creation of the Milk Carton Boat Races, which was an immediate hit. That first year the races had 1,200 entries who collectively used nearly 5,500 empty mill cartons in their fanciful, if not always seaworthy, aquatic vessels.

Almost thirty years later, in 1997, the event was still going strong, and *Life Magazine* published a two-page spread on the races with the headline "Aboard Good Ship Pasteurized." The article stated "the entries were as weird as they were imaginative. Would-be contestants rang doorbells and combed through garbage pails looking for empty containers"

Also in 1971, a parade of illuminated boats came up the Mississippi River to signal the start of the annual

Above: The Chinese Arch was added to Nicollet Mall in time for the 1970 Aquatennial, but moved the next year to the International Center at the State Fairgrounds.

Below: The Japanese-American float

Above: The recently revived Lake Harriet Street Car Line
Left: the Schlitz Forty–Horse Hitch from Milwaukee.

fireworks show. Roughly a hundred and fifty members of the American Indian Movement staged protests at the Torchlight Parade, arguing that some of the floats exploited and desecrated Indian culture and religion.

In 1972, a new Dance Line event provided opportunities for eight hundred girls from forty schools to display their talents. And that year Kuopio, Finland, became a sister city with Minneapolis as part of a national sister city initiative.

One of the most spectacular parade entries of 1973 was the Schlitz Forty—Horse Hitch from Milwaukee, Wisconsin, driven by Dick Sparrow. The enormous wagon was drawn by forty perfectly matched Belgian draught horses weighing 2000 pounds apiece. The moving sculpture of snorting beasts was 100 feet long.

The year 1973 was supercalafragalisticexpialidocious. What fun! Disneyland sent its Mary Poppins Float for the parades. Children screamed with delight.

Meanwhile, those festival attendees old enough to remember the old street car lines were hardly less delighted to take a ride on the newly extended Lake Harriet Line. The Minnesota Transportation Museum had been restoring old streetcars since 1962, and after the City of Minneapolis and the Minneapolis Park and Recreation Board acquired the original streetcar right-of-way between Lakewood Cemetery and Lake Harriet in 1970, the museum leased the land and began to run cars on a one-block stretch of track. By 1973, when the Aquatennial began to sponsor rides on the line, it had been extended to a mile.

Special guest Colonel Sanders piloted a riverboat float in both parades that year. And twenty Palestinian sympathizers protested Israeli and Lebanese participation in the Pageant of the Seven Seas events, without seriously disrupting them.

In 1974—here's the scoop!—The World's Largest Ice Cream Social was held at Loring Park featuring peppermint-striped tents and a box lunch auction. YIKES! They ran out of ice cream! Farrell's Ice Cream Parlor Restaurants had provided one thousand more pre-packaged ice cream bars than were planned for, but one hour after serving began they were gone.

Nicollet Avenue Mall became Main Street 1940 that year. People strolled along viewing antique store window displays of fashion and accessories from by-gone years. The streets were filled with antique cars. And the first annual Aquatennial Polkarama party was held at the Leamington Hotel. Contestants won trophies, prizes, and enjoyed professional dance exhibitions provided by David LaVay. Six bands kept everyone's feet moving: The Mroszinske Brothers, Dr. Lester Schuft, Florien Chimielewski, Rod Cerer, Wally Pikal, and The Polish Brass with Roger Stigney.

Meanwhile, downstream in Hastings, a glittering twilight parade of pleasure craft known as The Flotilla Frolic was held on the Mississippi River; more than sixty cruisers, pontoons, and houseboats festooned with decorative lights passed by, followed by a display of fireworks. Viewers called it "a moving light show that ended with a bang!" A new Aquatennial event was born.

A thousand dancers were expected at the Marityme Dance but two thousand showed up wearing nostalgic

Win Stephens and Tom Hastings

In Memoriam

The two principal founders of the Minneapolis Aquatennial, Tom Hastings and Win Stephens, both passed away in 1973. They were lifelong, faithful friends. Thomas Hastings served as Aquatennial President in 1940 and 1941, and Commodore in 1944 and 1945. Win Stephens was Commodore in 1940 and 1941. The contributions of these two men to the festival and the city were legion.

dancing duds. Don Cavitt's band and the Road Gang provided the music. Radio and television promotion, publicity, and public service programming for the Forties Flashback theme was considered the most successful to date. Total TV time was 433 minutes.

One highlight of the 1975 Aquatennial was the arrival of the Freedom Train at Minnehaha Park, as part of a cross-country tour in anticipation of the upcoming American Bicentennial. The train consisted of ten railroad cars crammed with artifacts and displays devoted to every aspect of American history. Mel and Betty Hatling hosted the five-day stop, during which 75,000 people paid a visit.

To complement the traveling museum, a series of heritage nights was presented at Minnehaha Falls. Six ethnic groups participated with one group featured each evening. Featured groups were Black Americans, Mexican and Spanish Americans, Scandinavians, Asians, Hawaiians, and Native Americans.

The Kenwood Hill Climb was revived in 1975, during which classic cars and motorcycles raced (or sometimes merely chugged) to the top of Kenwood Hill. The original event had been held in 1907. And a Skate-a-Thon was organized to raise money for the Long Prairie School Marching Band, which was scheduled to appear in the Pasadena Rose Parade near the float carrying that year's Queen of the Lakes, Anita Abraham, and Commodore Richard "Dick" Enroth.

In 1976, for the first time, four Princesses were chosen. Sheila Andrade, Pam Jasper, Susan Monahan, and Debra Kay Schmidt were thrilled to receive that honor; unfortunately, the program was discontinued the following year.

Another first in 1976 was a request for funds extended from the Aquatennial Board of Directors to the City Council to help underwrite new activities that had been added at a time when the economy as a whole was struggling with double-digit inflation. The theme that year was Summer of '76, and a Heritage of the Arts program showcased the work of 500 local artists. Viking football great Carl Eller was MC for the program's opening ceremony, and vintage cars were included as one of the art forms. The Wolverine Classic Jazz Orchestra provided music and a festival bus circled the city from Nicollet Island to the Walker and Guthrie to make it easier for patrons to see all the exhibits.

Also in 1976, in response to outspoken criticism from minority leaders, the Minneapolis Aquatennial Association adopted an affirmative action plan for both paid staff and volunteers to encourage more non-white participation in the festival. The Rose Parade float that year depicted the theme Minnesota Salutes Native Americans. The Marching M'bassadors from Long Prairie accompanied the float. They were only the third Minnesota band to be invited to make a Rose Parade appearance. But due to a mechanics' strike at United Airlines, they almost didn't make it. North Central Airlines came to their rescue by supplying 200 chartered seats!

In 1977, after seven years during which the Aquatennial theme highlighted other countries and cultures, organizers decided it was time for a Minnesota Homecoming, and celebrities with Minnesota roots were invited back to join in the Aquatennial fun. Among those who accepted invitations were Orville Freeman (Secretary of Agriculture during the Kennedy and Johnson administrations), TV anchorman Tom Brokaw, jazz keyboardist Bobby Lyle, and Kierkegaard scholar Paul Holmer.

Above: The Lake Calhoun Fish Fry

Right: The new IDS Tower above the Nicollet Mall Art Fair

Below: The 13K Open

Left: The Torchlight Parade was loud!

The heat at the Grande Day parade that year was almost unbearable. The temperature rose to 94 degrees with extremely high humidity, and more than a hundred marchers were treated for heat exhaustion.

Another bit of bad news was that thieves broke into the Leamington Hotel rooms of newly crowned Queen Sharolyn Frampton and Princess Janelle Urdahl and stole their jewelry. Police recovered the stolen property a few days later.

The official theme of the 1978 festival was Summer Break, though children were also made a special focus on July 29, when a Youth Parade marched down Marquette Avenue, the Junior Royalty were crowned, and various activities, including tug-of-wars and putt-putt-golf, were scheduled for Loring Park, Nicollet Mall, and a number of neighborhood venues.

The kilt-wearing Police Pipe Band of Winnipeg, Canada, played their bagpipes in both major parades, and the 34-member Bahamian National Police Force Band also appeared in their stylish red, white, and blue uniforms. Millionaire and philanthropist Percy Ross rode in the Torchlight Parade throwing $16,500 worth of silver dollars into the eager crowd.

Historic Nicollet Island was once again the site of the Heritage Festival where visitors could explore a melting pot of ethnic traditions and a potpourri of foods, watch craftsmen create and sell their wares, listen to folk music from around the world, and watch performances by native dancers from more than twenty nations.

The ever-popular Milk Carton Boat Races attracted 4,000 viewers and 1,400 participants. And a whopping eighty thousand spectators lined the shores of Lake Calhoun to see the Hydroplane Powerboat races. Fifty-five hydroplanes zoomed around the lake reaching speeds of 150 miles per hour. Due to the large number and boats and the quality of racers competing, the race obtained Grand Prix status for the first time that year.

That year the Long Prairie marching band was the Grand Champion Aqua parade winners for the tenth time. And for the first time, Senior Royalty were added to the Royal Party. Margaret Grimes proudly wore the crown as the first Senior Queen accompanied by the first Senior Commodore Stanley Antolak.

Another first that year—the Aquatennial hosted the World Open Powered Hang Glider Competition at the Gateway North Airport in Anoka.

Queens of the 1970s

Annette St. Dennis

Maureen Wagner

Deborah Wolinski

Patricia Kelzer

Barbara Peterson

Anita Abraham

Catherine Steinert

Kiki Rosatti

Sharolyn Frampton

Becky Rear

Above: Senior singers entertain the crowd.
Left: By the late 1970s, skateboarding had become a genuine Aquatennial sporting event. The sloping plaza of the Federal Reserve Building was a perfect venue.

In 1979 Mexico joined in the fun and festivities to help celebrate the Aquatennial's fortieth Anniversary. The Grande Day parade had a special guest—the Pillsbury Doughboy. This inflated figure measured 50 feet tall and 25 feet wide; it barely managed to fit under the skyway on Marquette Avenue between Sixth and Seventh streets during the parade.

Summer Break Youth Disco Dance had teens hustling, bumping, and grinding to the disco beat, while retired seniors from all walks of life who were active in the Old Guard Club, formed a new group, the Rocking Chair Brigade.

The newly formed Rocking Chair Brigade of Minneapolis helped to sell more than 15,000 Skipper Pins in 1979.

As the decade commenced, the Aquatennial theme was Welcome to the New World of the 80s, emphasizing the future rather than the past. Among the new activities introduced, Don and Robin Proud, directors of the Minneapolis branch of Scrabble Players, organized the first Aquatennial Scrabble competition.

Notable performances that year included the Edinburgh Society of Royal Country Dancers, Polynesian Paradise dancers and musicians, the Rong Shing Children's Chorus from Taiwan, a Jamaican Calypso troop, folk violinists from Vågå, Norway, a girls choir from Marseille, France, and the 41-member Kopervik Brass Band of Norway.

Al Zakariasen built a fourteen-foot-square, four-hole ice-fishing house shaped like a giant cream carton. It wasn't suitable for entry into the Milk Carton Boat races, but Cloverleaf Creamery generously donated funds and 3,300 empty cartons all the same.

Nicollet Mall once again played host to two successful art fairs in which 170 upper Midwest artists took part.

In 1981 Kuopio, Finland—sister city of Minneapolis—welcomed Aquatennial delegates, officials, and performers to renew the friendships between the

"Up, up and away!" Forty-nine colorful hot air balloons brightly lit the skies for ten thousand spectators in 1982.

two cities. Knott's Berry Farm of California put on a Western Revue with Wild West performances of can-can dancing, stuntmen, music and stage shows.

The parade theme the next year was "Show Tunes of America" featuring music from Broadway, movies and television. Festival parades included 150 units, 40 floats, 30 marching bands, 80 reigning and visiting queens. And spectators held their breath in awe (and sometimes their ears) as seven-hundred performers competed in the Aquatennial Brass Drum and Bugle competition in Parade Stadium.

Meanwhile, Senior Days, Family and Youth Days, and the Great American Flower and Garden Show welcomed citizens of the city. And down at Lake Calhoun, the Aquatennial entered the Guinness Book of World Records by making the world's largest root beer float.

Arthur Murray presented a Great American Dance Competition, and children screamed as they were "wowed" at the Big Bird Spectacular Amateur Show.

The U.S. Air Force Presidential Honor Guard Precision Drill Team made an appearance along with the US Army Reserve Colonial Color Guard.

The Kool Jazz Fest kicked off its national tour with trumpeter Maynard Ferguson and his big band, and vocalists Sarah Vaughan, Al Jarreau, and Shirley Witherspoon. Dixieland and gospel groups also performed.

Other musical shows were put on that year by the Jubilee, Watkins Barbershop Revue, the Mill City Gazette, and Knights of Harmony.

Mark King was commissioned to produce an oil painting, "Summer Break," depicting the Aquatennial. It was on display at several art shows. Postcards, prints,

Nicollet Mall, 1983. Aquatennial attendance reached new heights.

and posters were also available to the public.

Also in 1982, the roving units that had been popular in the 50s were revitalized under the rubric of The Great American Showtime. They entertained festival-goers at plazas and shopping centers throughout the metropolitan area.

A happy winner in the Sand Castle competition.

In 1983 both attendance at and participation in Aquatennial events surpassed all previous records. Two hundred fifty events took place, and volunteer participation also reach a high due to the enthusiastic participation of the Chicano community in response to the theme Mexico Magnifico. Three thousand volunteers participated. The Fiesta of the Americas took place July 16th in Loring Park. The centerpiece of festival design was a drawing of a stone calendar created by the sun worshipping Aztecs.

Cindy Williams Chandler became the first female General Festival Chairman that year. And the Kaiser Roll 10K race for wheelchair athletes was a more than welcome addition to athletic competitions.

In 1983 a sand castle competition was added to the festival. Each participant was given a 12' x 12' plot of sand on Lake Calhoun's North Beach to mold, etch, carve, pat, blow, and pack to create an amazing sculpture. Awards were presented in three categories— Sand Pail (under 16), Sand Castle (fun-loving adults), and Sand Sculpture (skilled artisans).

Formula One Grand Prix hydroplane racing was introduced on the Mississippi River upstream from the locks at St. Anthony Falls, replacing the hydroplane races held in previous years on Lake Calhoun. (Other water events were also moved from Lake Calhoun to Lake Nokomis because local residents were growing tired of the crowds and noise.) The Mississippi was also the setting for the Minneapolis River Run that year.

It rained during both major parades and driver Scott Teske spent hours vacuuming water out of the parade convertibles.

Later that year beloved Aquatennial Executive Director Ken Walstad passed away; he had served the festival faithfully and unstintingly for twenty-three years.

In 1984, ethnic themes were dropped in favor of a futuristic focus. Merkle, a radio-controlled robot, was the MC at the Queen's Coronation. The event, held at City Center, featured a laser light show synchronized to synthesized music.

Astronaut George "Pinky" Nelson of Willmar was Grand Marshall of the Grande Day and Torchlight parades. He had been in space on the Space Shuttle Challenger earlier that year.

Graphic design for the festival kept to the same futuristic theme, incorporating a computerized graphic of a sailboat on the water with the sun behind— even on the Skipper Pins.

New events included the City of Lakes Triathlon, a Family Bike Tour, an Amateur Talent Contest, and a Jazz Festival Under the Stars. The Milk Carton Boat Races were moved from Lake Calhoun to Lake Nokomis. And the Aqua Skipper Wheels, a new marching unit in the parades, featured fifty costumed escorts each carrying a three-foot skipper wheel on a streamer-decorated ten foot pole.

The festival remained popular, but in 1984 it lost more money than ever before in its forty-six-year history.

Championship frisbee-thrower Jose Montalvo from the Windy City Frisbee Club of Chicago

A welcome addition in 1985 was Sky of 10,000 Frisbees sponsored by Norwest Bank. One journalist wrote:

The sky over one of Minnesota's 10,000 lakes was a kaleidoscope of multi-colored plastic discs. They were tossed, thrown, sailed, and skimmed by some of the national's top freestyle players. The air looked like confetti as the audiences wowed to amazing dips, curves, hooks, and grabs. Even the dogs displayed their canine Frisbee antics.

That year an Illuminated Water Parade had more than thirty boats of various sizes wending their way from Kings' Cove through Hastings, Minnesota, passing the town levee and other viewing sites. From paddle boat to cabin cruiser to the smallest local runabout, all the vessels were illuminated, creating a moving light show reflected on the river waters, capped by a magnificent display of fireworks.

Lake Harriet's Queen of the Lakes paddleboat provided a glorious opportunity to spend a lazy, crazy, hazy day during Aqua summer.

Another event, Between Friends/Entre Amis, offered the opportunity for Minnesotans to learn more about their Canadian neighbors. The French-Canadians made an appearance with *Bonhomme Carnaval*, the seven-foot-tell snowman symbolizing the yearly Winter Carnival of Quebec. Three Canadian bands were featured in the Grande Day Parade. At Riverplace, on the east bank of the Mississippi River, re-enacters set up a voyageur fur-trading camp resembling the ones that might have existed in the early 1800's.

Above: Executive Director Kenneth Walstad
Right: Sailboats set for the Pepsi Sailing Regatta on Lake Calhoun.

Among the new events that year were a Ramblin' Raft Race on the Mississippi River and skydiving at Medicine Lake. And the twenty-sixth annual three-day Edina Swim Meet was held at the Edina Pool. Seven hundred athletes from England, Scotland, France, Canada, and the U.S. competed.

The Kenneth R. Walstad memorial award was established that year, to be presented annually to "the Aquatennial volunteer who, despite overwhelming challenges and impossible odds, most successfully contributes to the continuing vitality of the Minneapolis Aquatennial Association through the successful visionary execution of a continuing or new concept and/or program event, while, at the same time, maintaining the stability of the organization's financial and volunteer base."

The reflecting pool on the plaza at Northwestern Life Insurance was stocked with fish so youngsters with disabilities could take part in the fishing derby. They laughed at the Aqua Jesters antics at the same time experiencing the excitement of reeling in their big catch.

And forty hot air balloons from the Upper Midwest and Canada colored the skies. A hundred sailboats were expected at the traditional Sailing Regatta on Lake Calhoun, which was celebrating its thirty-seventh year.

With losses mounting, and rising liability insurance fees, in 1986 the Aquatennial reduced the number of events. The theme that year was Salute to Liberty. Woodcarver Steve Dow created a magnificent seventeen-foot replica of the Statue of Liberty which was displayed in the Crystal Court of the IDS tower.

Teens took eagerly to the Skateboard Jam held on the shores of Lake Calhoun. Soaring high was winner Greg Dahn. And a 50' by 50' Monopoly board was created in the courtyard of Ridgedale Mall, with proceeds dedicated to the Muscular Dystrophy Association.

In 1986 Rebecca Planer was in her third year as the only female to wear the uniform of Vice Commodore. Skipper Pins were available in two versions—the standard plastic and a new cloisonné pin.

The Aqua Jester committee produced the wonderfully creative coloring book of clowns clowning around for their fortieth anniversary. It included color photos of the funny looking clowns, some with a red nose, big feet, and tiny hat. The coloring book committee consisted of Harry C. Powers, Steve Howland, Bob Howland, Kelli Waalk, and Jerry Waalk of Bolger Publications, Inc.

Minneapolis Mayor Donald M. Fraser proclaimed July 19, 1986, as Minneapolis Aqua Jester Day and Governor Rudy Perpich sent warmest wishes.

Unfortunately, 1986 was the last year of the Skipper Pin promotion, "Guess the Queen Contest." Over the years

At the 1985 American League All-Star Game, from left to right: Brenda Schuler, Princess; Dave Anton; Lori Grote, Queen; Mark LaVelle; Janet Schotzko, Princess; Skip Nelson.

winners had received countless prizes of convertibles, trips, shopping excursions, and cash.

On one afternoon during the next year's festivities, a record nine inches of rain and high winds forced the Minneapolis-St. Paul airport to close. Tornadoes were predicted. Attendees at the Queen of the Lakes coronation at International Market Square that night were "held hostage" by the flooding.

Also in 1987, employees of the J.B. Hudson

Above: A weightlifting demonstration

Below: The Swinging Squares of Bloomington show their stuff on Peavey Plaza

Company discovered two Queen of the Lakes coronation crowns (worn in 1942 and 1948) in the company's storage vault. Company president Melvin W. Schmidt returned them to the Aquatennial Association.

An Aqua Treasure Quest was innaugurated that year, and for the fourth year the U.S. Swim and Fitness triathlon was held along Minnehaha Parkway and around Lake Nokomis, with 1,500 women and men participating, with proceeds going to the Muscular Dystrophy Association.

Minneapolis Mayor Donald Fraser proclaimed one day during the festival as Snow White Day. The Disney film had recently been re-released, fifty years after the original screening, and a birthday party was staged at Lake Harriet with Mickey Mouse, Pluto, Goofy, Captain Hook and Dopey attending. Fifteen hundred radio stations nationwide did a simulcast broadcast of the song "Whistle While You Work."

The "Bach, Boats, and Broadway" series was performed by the Bach Society chorus that year, and the Minneapple River Run, a 5.5 mile run finishing at Riverplace, remained popular. The run included seven categories with six age groups and a wheelchair division. Everyone who completed went home with a Minneapple T-shirt.

Senior King W.C. "Bing" Crosby told the newspaper his favorite event was the Senior Prom because he could convince about 700 men to come to the dance and every lady would have a partner. The Torchlight Parade, sponsored by KARE 11 TV, was upgraded that year to attract national television networks.

The Champion Spark Plug Powerboat Classic on the Mississippi River was open to a broad range of watercraft in 1987, unlike the Formula One races held the previous four years. And Cal Lueneburg, Mr. Minnesota, brought bulging biceps and defined deltoids to

50th Anniversary Queen of the Lakes Barbara Stockdill rides "The Dragon," recently purchased from the Rose Parade Association

display at the State Body Building Championships at Northrop Auditorium. The event featured bodybuilders and their awesome physiques against backdrops of sounds, light, special effects, and big screen videos.

Queen of the Lakes Sandy Polesky (1987) graced the majestic and impressive float "The Dragon," which had been recently purchased from the Pasadena Rose Parade Association. The float sashayed majestically

The 80s

down the avenue while snorting puffs of smoke. It was a crowd pleaser! The Parade Division had stripped the float down and rebuilt it when it arrived in Minneapolis. All mechanical problems were fixed including the hydraulics and smoke machine. Then Bob Labrech, Angus Down, Bonnie McDonald, Randy and Sharon Englland, Louis Ryg, and other volunteers worked long hours painting and glittering the outside. They dedicated the float to Ken Walstad, former Aquatennial executive director.

In 1988, Twin Cities Pee Wee and Cub baseball teams participated in much needed summer ball thanks to Aquatennial's Youth Baseball Classic. Hundreds of kids from thirty-two teams participated in the tournament. Each player received a souvenir trophy and a variety of team awards were also distributed.

That year the Skateboard Jam featured 300 skaters showing their best stuff to over 25,000 spectators. Some of the thrilling teen "boarders" had aspirations of turning pro.

At the Dancin' in the Streets and Cheepskates of Minnesota events, break dancers and roller skaters held audiences in awe with their callisthenic abilities.

Skipper Pin sales nearly tripled in 1988 as people scrambled to qualify for the Summer Fantasy Home Giveaway. One finalist was announced daily on KARE 11 TV's 10 p.m. newscasts, and given a house key. On the last day of the Aquatennial, the daily winners gathered near Shakopee to try their keys in the lock of a home valued at $120,000. Judy Orne's worked. A fifty-six-year-old widow who had been transferred to Minneapolis from Kentucky by her company, Ms. Orne was then living with her daughter.

That year the Torchlight Parade telecast was syndicated across the United States for the first time to eight major markets, including Washington D.C., Phoenix, Boston, and Denver. And for the first time, real torches were used to enhance the dazzle and mystery of the passing floats.

Just prior to the Grande Day Parade, families were encouraged to join in a three-mile walk along West River Parkway. Everyone who came received a T-shirt, and the first thousand entrants received free seating at the parade.

At another event, high school marching bands from across the nation competed for cash prizes. The Alexandria High School band won.

Mary Jo Dillenburg

Cathy Linsmier

Lorrie Werness

Amy Mertes

Jody Hempel

Lori Grote

Julie Melin

Sandra Polesky

Jennifer Tolrud

Barbara Stockdill

In its fiftieth year, Aquatennial organizers staged a free evening of the arts called Arts on the Avenue, featuring shows by some of the best visual, performing, and literary arts the region had to offer on more than fifty staging areas along First Avenue. More than ten thousand people came to "oooh and aaah."

The Skipper Pin promotion featured a dream prize of "a $10,000 shopping spree" compliments of Norwest Banks. And fifty 14K gold Fiftieth Anniversary Aquatennial Skipper Pins were produced in honor of the festival milestone—a crowning touch to any Skipper Pin collection. Each sold for $500.

John Kleber, a Minneapolis-based printermaker and designer, created an Aqua Follies-inspired billboard illustration to commemorate the anniversary. It was posted near the intersection of 7th Street and 5th Avenue downtown, with an additional fifteen facimiles displayed throughout the city.

Phyllis George, 1971 Miss America and NFL sportscaster, was the Grand Marshall in the Torchlight Parade.

The Sand Castle event drew more than seven hundred entrants eager to play on the beach, and more than two thousand golfers entered the Aquatennial's new Crystal Light Million Dollar Hole-in-One Golf Tourney, where prizes were given away daily.

The Mississippi River Showcase at Boom Island, a fund raiser for International Summer Olympics, featured food, light shows, and an impressive line-up of entertainers including the Pointer Sisters, the Oak Ridge Boys, Christopher Reeve, and the 1989 Miss America—Anoka's own Gretchen Carlson.

The Skateboard Jam needed two additional ramps to accommodate a hundred additional skaters. More than three-hundred contestants "caught air" in the competition which also welcomed professional skateboarder Kevin Staab.

A Batmobile, a Winnebago camper ("Crappy Hamper"), a Rubber Dickie, and a giant bug "Twentipeded" were among the ninety five Milk Carton Boat Races entries that year.

The 50th Anniversary parades were two miles long—three miles shorter than the inaugural parade of 1940. Three-thousand dancers enjoyed a gorgeous open air party at Dancing in the Moonlight on the Hennepin County Government Center Plaza.

At the coronation, royal parties of the past were introduced on stage, year by year, as part of the anniversary celebration. When it was over, volunteers congratulated one another on a "job well done" and let out a huge sigh of relief.

Unfortunately, the 50th Anniversary Festival experienced a substantial deficit.

MAKING WAVES

In 1990, Aquatennial planned to partner with Kemps Ice Cream to create a special festival ice cream flavor. The sixty piece Heartland of America band wowed audiences, and the Plaza Tennis Invitational, held downtown, attracted tennis aficionados and curious urban workers on their lunch break alike.

Duane "Buttons" Kemna passed away in 1990. He was the Skipper Pin salesman of all salesmen. In 1989 he topped the charts, selling 3,400 pins on Nicollet Mall.

In 1991, more than six-hundred youngsters braved the rainy weather to march around the Metrodome's field on Twins Salute to Aquatennial Night, prior to a game against the Boston Red Sox. Rousing music was provided by the Irondale Marching Band, the Royal Party sang "Take Me Out to the Ballgame" during the seventh-inning stretch, and Aqua Jesters added their merriment to the proceedings.

And Nancy Wettstein from Bloomington was the grand prize winner in a contest sponsored by Target, giving her the opportunity to shop 'til she dropped before taking a trip for two to Cancun, Mexico.

In 1992, the Grande Day Parade was moved from the first weekend of the celebration to the second weekend in order to tie into the themes of Family Fun Day. Many felt that the parade suffered as a result of this move because many high school bands ended their summer schedules after the Torchlight Parade and skipped the second parade.

In an event held at the Nicollet Island Pavilion—Minnesota Goes Platinum—the Aquatennial organizers honored those who had been involved in staging six major sports events in Minnesota the previous year. Representatives of these events also served as honorary Grand Marshalls in the Torchlight Parade. Reed MacKenzie represented the United States Golf Association, which had held the U.S. Open at Hazeltine in 1991; Irwin Jacobs, the International Special Olympics; Carl Pohlad, the World Series; Marilyn Nelson, Super Bowl XXVI; McKinley Boston, the JCAA Final Four; and Chris Voelz, the NCAA Women's Gymnastics Championships. It was a once-in-a-lifetime event. The "big six" and 600 other guests viewed a multi-media presentation showcasing each producer's event.

On a more modest scale than these grand events, the Aquatennial staged its first annual Croquet Tournament on the lawn outside Lincoln Center downtown, with benefits going to the International Hearing Foundation.

A gelatin slide (with benefits going to the Leukemia Society) took place at Lake Nokomis. Sliders came fully "costumed" and with their own cheering

A platoon of marchers pushing signature red Target carts

sections. All who contributed $75 went down the slide and landed in a thousand gallons of cold, gooey AQUA gelatin.

Target Corporation sponsored both major parades in 1992, and more than a hundred employees in each parade pushed signature red Target shopping carts. The audiences loved the concept, and it became a parade staple for years. The Torchlight Parade that year was the coldest in parade history, with temperatures plunging to the 50's.

The sale of Skipper Pins also plummeted, perhaps because fewer people shopped downtown or associated the festival with genuinely charitable causes. (Or maybe it was because fireworks weren't on the schedule!)

To combat waning enthusiasm, the Aquatennial unveiled a new official "mark" that became a part of each year's theme logo. It was designed by the Kuester Group, an award winning design firm in Minneapolis, as part of a "branding" effort to give the festival more continuity and name recognition year-to-year.

In 1993, four different Skipper Pin buttons were offered featuring the "GetCoolGetTogether" theme. A standard pin cost $3.00. A more colorful one with a blinking light cost twice as much. For ten dollars you could get a classic cloisonné pin, and for a hundred dollars collectors could purchase a larger cloisonné pin, individually numbered on the back.

Tetra Pak, a Swedish packing company with offices in Minneapolis, used twenty-five thousand milk cartons to make a hundred-foot boat in the shape of an aircraft carrier, in honor of those who had served in Operation Desert Storm. Nearly 150 people rode on the boat.

In 1993 the first ever Aquatennial jazz festival was held. It was a free, two-day event, encompassing not only jazz but also more popular genres such as reggae, rock, rap, blues, and country. It made a big splash!

Proud historic automobile enthusiasts and collectors displayed their grand beauties at the Concours d'Elegance at Lake Nokomis. And James R. "Jamie" Lowe III became the youngest president in the history of the festival at the age of twenty-nine. The Timberwolves came aboard Aqua's event schedule for the first time, hosting a three-day clinic in basketball fundamentals for three hundred kids—kindergarten through eighth grade.

That year John Brant, a member of the U of M Alumni Marching Band, marched in his twenty-second consecutive Aquatennial parade. The next year Brant became Vice Commodore of Parades, and in 2003 he served as Commodore. He was always looking for music that was exciting and different. "Marching bands breathe life into a parade. It's the emotions involved in music that make it so exciting, unpredictable and spontaneous." He witnessed this phenomenon first hand while marching in a Torchlight Parade with the Alumni Band. When they began playing the Minnesota Rouser, he saw a man in a wheelchair struggling to stand. "It's like live theater—the crowd doesn't just watch it, they experience it."

Six local water skiers from Ski American planned to ski the Mississippi River from Minneapolis to the Gulf of Mexico in less than twelve days, breaking the record. They had to ski the entire trip together, fanned out behind the boat, fully aware that south of St. Louis hazardous chemicals and sewage would be an ever-increasing threat.

The Mississippi also figured into a less demanding event called Rubber Ducky. Anyone could sponsor a duck by purchasing a "duck number." At the sound of the shotgun blast, fifteen thousand rubber ducks were let loose from the Boom Site to paddle, swim, or float downstream to the finish line near the Nicollet Island pavilion. The first twenty quackers to cross the line won wonderful prizes for their owners.

As part of the celebration in 1994, Minnesota artist Anthony "Tony" Whelihan created an extravagant watercolor called "Splendiferous." He also designed the standard $3.00 Aquatennial Skipper Pin along with two special high quality cotton T-shirts. One featured the 1994 pin logo and the other an illustration of the Minneapolis skyline.

The festival headquarters moved that year to Riverplace, just across the Mississippi River from downtown, after having spent twelve years in the old Warren Cadillac space near Parade Stadium. The festival's first office, back in 1939, was in the Builders Exchange. Later it was moved to 529 Palace Building, then 115 South Fifth, 210 South Tenth, and the old Minneapolis Convention and Visitors Bureau's location downtown.

After a one-year absence, fireworks once again effervesced and sparkled on the Mississippi waters, thanks to LaCroix Sparkling Water. And the Skipper Pin Sweepstakes brought squeals of delight to two lucky winners. Elsie Grivna had never won anything in her life. Now she had her choice of a trip to Disney World or a $1,000 Target shopping Spree. She chose to shop. So a limousine carried Elsie, Aqua President Bob Jaskowiak, and Queen Sara Borg to the Brooklyn Park Target Greatland. The other Target shopping winner was Phil Ratte of Coon Rapids.

In 1995 Ken Hafften stepped proudly into the newly created position of Aquatennial Captain. And Frank Anton, a Minneapolis native, celebrated thirty-five years of Aqua involvement in many capacities. Bravo, Frank! The Aqua Jesters chocked up a half-century of glorious clowning. And QVC, a cable channel devoted to shopping from home, broadcast the Torchlight Parade live. It was watched by millions of viewers across the nation who also got the chance to buy twenty Minnesota-made products from the comfort of their living room sofas.

For many years Aqua royalty and staff had been riding in style thanks to Pontiac. In 1995 Pontiac donated the use of twelve convertibles—six Firebirds and six Trans Ams—three transport Mini Vans, and three Bonnevilles.

Dayton's sponsored an astounding fireworks display that year. One observer wrote:

AAAHHH! AMAZING! The festival grand finale was ablaze over the Stone Arch Bridge with reflections sparkling on the water of the Mississippi. The show was set to music, compliments of Cities '97. Zambelli International, creators of pyrotechnic displays all over the world designed an unforgettable show for an unforgettable evening; a celebration of community spirit. "The the world renowned Zambelli family, known as "the first family of fireworks," are known as "most creative and innovative pyrotechnics in the world." These pyrotechnic wizards produce 2,000 shows annually, 800 alone on the Fourth of July. Their Aqua production uses 10,000 pounds of explosives and 45 miles of wire.

Dayton's Target division sponsored the Grande Day and Torchlight parades. A fifty-five-foot inflatable Indy Car sat on 28 Target shopping carts pushed by Target employees. And the second annual Skipper Open was held at Pheasant Run Golf Course followed by dinner at Mama D's.

The pool of Aquatennial volunteers continued to show amazing strength and commitment. According to an informal survey of vice-commodores, 1,840 people spent more than 17,000 hours volunteering for the festival during the 1994-1995 cycle. "That's the equivalent of eight full-time employees working year-round," said Jamie Lowe, Chief Operating Officer of the festival.

Without volunteers and donations, the Aquatennial would have cost the city more than fifteen million dollars to produce. Long days and nights of hard work with nary a paycheck in sight. It's the life of a volunteer. Hats off to them!

In 1996, a portion of the proceeds from the 5K Torchlight Dusk Run was donated to the Bob Allison Ataxia Research Center. The race drew more entries than ever before. That same year, a thousand Aquatennial Commemorative Lithographs were commissioned by the Minneapolis Optimist Club. Each vibrantly colored print was numbered and signed by artist Tom Casmer. Proceeds from these first annual prints benefitted the Minneapolis Optimists Kitchi-Kahniss Youth Facility.

Three hundred street rods from MSRA Street Rod Car Show converged on Main Street near Riverplace that year. And for the first time, sign language was provided for the hearing impaired at the Queen of the Lakes Coronation.

Downtown Minneapolis started rockin' at noon on Block E prior to the Torchlight Parade with live music from a myriad of popular local bands.

The Commodore in 1996 was Charlie Boone, known throughout Minnesota (then as now) as a member of Boone and Erickson, one of the most successful partnerships in Minnesota Radio.

Boone's association with the Aquatennial stretches back to the very beginnings, as this recollection testifies:

Thousands of people have memories of our Aquatennial. Mine are both professional and personal. In 1959, Randy Merriman, a national TV star, returned to Minnesota and served as Commodore. On a trip to Winnipeg to view their festival, he heard a radio voice in Fargo. I was that voice and that Aquatennial changed my life. I joined WCCO radio in the summer of 1959 and after 52 years, retired in 2010.

When Bill Popp asked me to succeed him as Commodore in 1996, what could I say but yes! I had a great experience getting to know the many communities in Minnesota.

The Duck Race on the Mississippi once again attracted thousands of entries. All of the twenty thousand ducks set afloat were eligible to win prizes for those who had chosen them, but four had been designated as "million dollar ducks." No one knew which four these were, but had any one of them crossed the finish line among the first four, it would have meant a million-dollar payoff for the lucky sponsor.

Charlie Boone surrounded by Aqua Jesters

At the Milk Carton race, now dubbed a "people-powered water race," Charlie Casserly took home the trophy for the fourth time.

In 1997, the Aquatennial adopted a new slogan to be used every year—The Best Ten Days of Summer. That same year Robin Plaistad became the first female Aquatennial Captain, and the festival shifted its focus from quantity to quality, scaling back the number of events to forty.

Aquatennial legend Bob Stanek, affectionately known as "Rags," died that year. He'd been an Aqua Jester since 1956, and had appeared in seventy-eight Aqua parades, jousting and jesting. Among his countless awards was Aqua Jesters Clown of the Year. The Jesters had dedicated parades to him in 1994 by wearing picture buttons of him and designing posters to commemorate his life. He brought thousands of laughs and smiles over the years.

Among the questions fielded by Aqua office staff were these:

A. *I live in Brooklyn Center. If I sit in my car, how much of the water ski show can I see?*

B. *Where can I park so that I can lay in the top bunk of my camper and watch the parade?*

C. What kind of cards do they play in the "500" Card Tournament?

D. I love to watch the Torchlight Parade, but I work at night. Do you think you could change the parade to Saturday night?

These questions are for real.

Tennis pros associated with the Inner City Tennis Legends program conducted clinics for inner city youth and other local players. Breakfast groups discussed tennis strategies, and kids played lots of tennis, and some got to play exhibition matches with the sports legends.

The Minnesota Orchestra, with Eiji Oue at the podium, performed on the last night of the festival an hour before the fireworks finale, once again sponsored by Dayton's.

In 1998, Smashing Pumpkins regaled a crowd of a hundred thousand at the Aquatennial Block Party. The Aquatennial Director's Award for Excellent Events was awarded to the Senior Alumni. And the volunteer award was renamed the Steven K. Anderson Memorial Volunteer of the Year Award, in honor of Steve Anderson, who had recently passed away. Steve had volunteered in many capacities for the festival: Captain, 1996 festival; Chairman of the Volunteer Management Committee, Sports and Lakes Vice Commodore, as well as chief ambassador visiting many cities throughout the region promotion Minneapolis' Official Civic Celebration. Everything he did was "smartly done!" (His favorite phrase)

In 1999 Dennis Schulstad, a Brigadier General in the U.S. Air Force, took on the added duties associated with serving as Aquatennial President. Using his many connections, Schulstad arranged for the Air Force Heartland of America Band came to town to perform concerts during Aquatennial and participate in the Torchlight Parade.

One of the most memorable events that year took place in an elegantly staged affair on the top floor of the tallest building in Minnesota, the IDS tower. Bob Cabana, a Minneapolis native, welcomed all the Ambassadors, queen candidates, and visiting dignitaries, and regaled them with tales of his experiences as a Marine test pilot and later an astronaut who participated in four space shuttle missions and commanded two of them.

Queens of the 1990s

Jennifer Munson

Lisa Gratz

Brenda Flury

Kacie Cassidy

Robyn Johnson

Sara Borg

Bethany Hibbard

Christine Scherping

Carrie Nevitt

Kelly Gahlon

The 90s

The start of the Stand Up for Avenues Paddleboard Race, 2013

At the dawn of the new century, Aquatennial organizers issued a new vision statement:

The Minneapolis Aquatennial builds partnerships to create events and relationships that serve and represent the unity and diversity of Minneapolis and the state through serious play to create wonderful memories and glorious opportunities.

There was nothing really "new" about the vision, but the civic ideals of the festival are always worth reiterating, especially at times when the commitment is on the brink of faltering.

In 2000, Donna Erickson became the first woman to serve as Aquatennial President and the first woman inducted into the Aquatennial Admirals Club, the alumni group for Aquatennial Past Presidents and Commodores.

Centerpoint Energy put forth their energy to sponsor the beautifully illuminated Torchlight Parade. And the Skipper Pin design honored the 30th anniversary of the Milk Carton Boat Races.

Nearly 2,500 people attended the inaugural Salsa Street Dance in the Lyn-Lake area. The festivities included food, free dance instructions, and music by the

Fans await the Torchlight Parade.

hug to all of you for representing the festival with such style and grace.

Aquatennial enthusiasts also witnessed the final Grande Day Parade that year. In fact, the festival itself underwent a major overhaul, with the Aquatennial name and events (except the Queen of the Lakes program) becoming the responsibilty of the Minneapolis Downtown Council. Meanwhile, an Aquatennial Ambassadors Organization (AAO) was formed as a non-profit entity to continue the tradition of royalty/ambassadors outreach into leadership and volunteer roles. (See more on page 126.)

But such administrative horse-trading had little effect on the two-day party held at Parade Stadium—temporarily renamed Aquatennial Village—that year, featuring live music for all ages (including the Minnesota Orchestra), arts and crafts, baseball tournaments, carnival rides, refreshment stands and a beer garden.

In 2002 the Hennepin History Museum (HHM) proudly announced that it had become the official repository for the Historic Aquatennial Collection. Since then the Past Queens Association has been the official sponsor of the archives.

That year, for the first time in the parade history, the illuminated Torchlight Parade was cancelled due to heavy rain and severe lightning. With the Grande Day Parade now temporarily in moth balls, the 2002 Queen of the Lakes, Natalie Neubauer, earned the unfortunate distinction of being the only Queen never to have appeared in an Aquatennial parade during her official reign.

Past Queen of the Lakes Lisa Renee Gratz (1991),

continued on page 129

Latin Sounds. Verizon Wireless provided free international calls connecting the community to the world.

In 2001, Nancy Lindahl became the first female Aquatennial Commodore. Sadly, the Junior Royalty program was disbanded after this year. A huge Aquatennial

2002 - THE FESTIVAL REORGANIZES

by Robert Perkins,
Dennis Schulstad, and Donna Erickson

Over the years, the character of the Aquatennial has changed, as events have been added, expanded, or eliminated. The one consistent issue, year after year, has been to raise enough money to continue producing a high quality festival.

The Minneapolis Aquatennial Association (Aquatennial) and the Saint Paul Winter Carnival (Carnival) were each running their own operations. Each had paid staff and rental office space. Some years, the Aquatennial would be in excellent financial shape while the Carnival was deeply in debt—especially when the weather did not cooperate for their signature ice castle. At other times, the Carnival did well while the Aquatennial was in debt. Over the years, there were discussions that the two operations should be merged into a single paid staff and office. For various reasons, that did not materialize.

After experiencing more than a decade of financial insecurity, the Aquatennial entered the twenty-first century in severe financial difficulty. Aquatennial was no longer financially viable under the model that had been used for many years. There were many reasons for this, including the lack of any monetary assistance from the City of Minneapolis (other than some police support for events). Aquatennial relied on revenue from communities that were sponsoring Queen of the Lakes candidates, from corporations, and from individual donors. The community festivals continued to send candidates, but were facing their own financial challenges and could not afford to pay more in entry fees. Many local businesses, struggling to remain competitive in a challenging economic environment, either reduced or eliminated their donations. The generous individuals who reached into their own pockets each year were getting tired of endless requests for money. Efforts were made to reduce overhead by trimming staff, office space, and travel to festivals outside of Minnesota, without undercutting the festival's appeal, but many bills were overdue and even the company that produced the exceptional fireworks was owed thousands of dollars. It became obvious that extreme action was needed to save the festival.

After extensive discussion by the board of directors and other leaders, it was decided that only two viable options remained. One was to declare bankruptcy and call it quits for the Aquatennial. The other was to find a new organization with the financial wherewithal to assume control. The Minneapolis Downtown Council (DTC) was the logical choice. The most popular Aquatennial events—the fireworks, parade, sand castle contest, milk carton races, and river activities—attracted tens of thousands of people to downtown Minneapolis. The DTC had the capability to make the events financially successful since they already had the staff and expertise to run events like Holidazzle and the Hennepin Avenue Block Party. The DTC also included among their membership almost all of the sponsor companies for those events.

There were long and difficult negotiations involving some of the leaders of DTC and Aquatennial, such as John Bergquist (City of Minneapolis), Ted Cadwell (legal counsel), Rick Collins (former Aquatennial President), Todd Klingel (DTC rep and Aquatennial board member), Bob Perkins (former Aquatennial President) and Denny Schulstad (former Aquatennial President and Commodore).

In the end, the DTC purchased all Aquatennial events and assets, except the Ambassador Program, and Marketing Minneapolis, LLC, a division of the Minneapolis Downtown Council, assumed all of the Aquatennial's debts. The Ambassador Program, which the Aquatennial Board of Directors considered an essential element of the festival, was to be continued by a new group of volunteers, the Aquatennial Ambassador Organization (AAO). This reorganization of responsibilities rescued the Aquatennial and allowed it to continue with great confidence into the future.

AQUATENNIAL AMBASSADOR ORGANIZATION (AAO)

Following approval of the asset sale by the Aquatennial Board of Directors, the Aquatennial Ambassador Organization (AAO) was formed and incorporated as a nonprofit on November 30, 2001. The first organizational meeting of AAO was held on December 5, 2001. The newly formed nonprofit qualified for and received 501(c)(3) tax-exempt status as a charitable and educational entity under which contributions by individuals became deductible to the extent allowed by law. Tax-exempt status had not been possible under the previous model.

Similar to other festivals around the country, the Aquatennial Ambassador program began operating as a separate volunteer organization. Aquatennial ambassadors and the Queen of the Lakes candidate program were coordinated by the newly formed AAO and managed by veteran Aquatennial alumni. The first AAO Board of Directors meeting was held on January 31, 2002. The 2002 AAO Board of Directors included: John Bergquist, Jack Breese, Charlie Boone, John Brant, Donna Erickson, Tamara Fleischhaker, Lisa Gratz, Joe Johnston, Richard Kloos, Janet Kramer, Nancy Lindahl, Dennis McGrath, Fran Murnane, Carrie Nevitt, Jennifer Onnen, Bob Perkins, Kiki Rosatti, Denny Schulstad, and Harley Wells.

Meanwhile, beginning with the 2002 Aquatennial festival, the DTC assumed the helm and began producing the major events. The DTC and the AAO worked closely together to continue traditions and create new ones. The possibilities that these changes posed were exciting, as well as challenging, for all who believed in the Aquatennial experience and its influence on the quality, distinction, and vitality of our community life. For the alumni who enjoyed the benefits of great and lasting friendships, attention turned to ensuring that the Aquatennial Ambassador program was preserved for generations to come.

The AAO continues to instill knowledge, skills, and confidence in young women to enable them to become leaders in their fields. The AAO also works to preserve, maintain, and promote relationships among Aquatennial alumni. Many Aquatennial alumni continue to make generous monetary gifts to help dedicated volunteers perpetuate a legacy rich in history, camaraderie, and integrity.

AQUATENNIAL PRINCESSES

Princess Anne Sumangil and Princess Juliane Borg - 2001

Each year since 1952, two fortunate young ladies haave been chosen to be Aquatennial Princesses. They are a splendid complement to the Queen of the Lakes, and the three make a distinguished royal trio. The Princesses represent the City of Minneapolis and the festival with distinguished pride and honor. They frequently make individual appearances throughout Minnesota and share responsibilities with the Queen regarding festival representation and the presentation of the Commodore's Award to deserving community volunteers.

The Past Princess Association fosters a sense o community among the Princesses through networking professional support, and social events. It's a place fo them to nurture friendships within the framework o the Aquatennial bond they share. Each year one Pas Princess serves as a Queen-of-the-Lakes judge, an many have served as judges in other community fes tivals. The legacy of the Aquatennial Princesses is o service through volunteerism and ambassadorship i mentoring and leadership.

served as Aquatennial President for both 2002 and 2003, following in the footsteps of trailblazing Queen Donna Erickson, mentioned earlier.

In 2002 the Aquatennial hosted the biggest celebration of aviation history in the state's history, as fifty vintage aircraft arrived from around the country, along with nearly a hundred of aviation's Living Legends and some 25,000 aviation lovers. Notable guests included the Flying Tigers, Black Sheep Squadron, Doolittle Raiders, Tuskegee Airmen, and Pearl Harbor survivors. Saturday night was an "Evening with Eagles."

And the Aquatennial Plaza Tennis Invitational held its eighth annual tournament.

In 2003 the Hennepin History Museum inaugurated the tradition of mounting a Aquatennial exhibit every year. The first was called Historic Aquatennial – A Media Perspective. And that year, after a year's hiatus, the Grande Day Parade returned, under the sponsorship of U.S. Bank, with the theme "A Community MOSAIC." A fun—and educational—treasure hunt was held on a Saturday at the IDS Crystal Court, during which kids were able to hunt through a coin mural made up of more than 500,000 pennies. Specially marked coins were redeemable for prizes, and the 50th floor observatory was opened that day for viewing the cities.

The theme of the Torchlight Parade was "Red Hot, Cool Blue"—hot being summer days, cool blue the city's abundant open waters. Ann Bancroft, a Minnesota native who

Above: Volleyball at Lake Calhoun.

Below: A band entertains the crowd before the fireworks get underway.

More than two thousand athletes from around the world vie for a half-million dollars in prizes each year in the Life Time Fitness

Triathlon. The event consists of a 1.5K swim, a 40K bike race, and a 10K run on a beautiful course through the Twin Cities.

was the first woman to cross the ice to both the North and South Poles, was the Grand Marshal of the Torchlight Parade.

More than forty volleyball teams competed at the Emer'gen-C Co-ed Beach Volleyball Tournament at Lake Calhoun's volleyball courts. Ron Shara held a workshop offering fishing tips at the same lake.

Aquatennial turned 65 in 2004, and featured 65 events for all ages to enjoy.

Cub Foods sponsored a Festival of Neighborhoods

event during which sixteen Minneapolis parks were alive with neighbors, free food, fun, and entertainment at specified dates during the Aqua week. The Life Time Fitness Triathlon featured a timing format known as "the Equalizer" which allowed professional men and women to compete on equal ground. At stake was the $500,000 purse with the winner winning half. Not bad for a day's work! Eighteen Olympic winners were in the race which was covered by NBC television.

In a rule change applauded by some and derided by others, Easy Handle Milk Cartons were now allowed in the Kemps Milk Carton Boat Race along with the traditional wax-coated paper cartons. Kemps also offered 102 free milk cartons to all contest entrants.

As part of the annual Beach Bash in 2004, a Penny Frenzy was held. A million pennies were delivered to the south shore of Lake Calhoun by armored truck and dumped to create a giant penny-filled sandbox. The first two thousand children to participate received a free TCF Penny Frenzy Piggy Bank. But what they were really after was one of the ten thousand collector pennies in the mix, and the specially marked coins that could be redeemed for special prizes.

Wilderness Inquiry brought experienced canoe instructors to Lake Calhoun to guide paddlers of all ages and abilities in individualized thirty-minute training sessions.

The Grande Day Parade celebrated "Many

An Aqua Jester entertains the crowd

Worlds—Past and Present." The past was represented by more than twenty Veterans of Foreign Wars posts from around Minnesota, led by District Commander Stan Kowalski. The present was represented by the Minneapolis Mosaic, a progam dedicated to honoring the diversity and cultural heritage of local communities. The Torchlight Parade theme, "A Night of a Million Stars" featured seventy-five authentic torches alongside the CenterPoint Energy Minnegasco float, sponsors for the parade.

In 2005, new events were introduced to emphasize the "Aqua" in Aquatennial. The North Mississippi Regional Park along with Minneapolis Park & Rec hosted the first two-day log rolling competition, environmental activities, a climbing wall, historical re-enactments,

The F1 Powerboat Races

shoreline of Lake Calhoun.

Forty states and twelve countries were represented at the Life Time Fitness Triathlon in 2005, which, as usual, welcomed swarms of spectators. The event featured an Olympic distance, 1.5K swim, 40K bike and 10K fun on a beautiful course through the Twin Cities. More than two thousand triathletes from around the world participated. An interactive area for kids was set up at Lake Nokomis near the swim start with inflatables, football and basketball games, face painters, and a big screen TV's to watch the races. NBC Sports re-broadcast the triathlon at 2:00 the same day.

The U.S. Bank's "Volunteers Shine" float featured riders who were award-winning volunteers from the company's Volunteers Shine program.

The Target Fireworks were orchestrated to the theme "Rock and Roll Spectacular," with the soundtrack broadcast live on KOOL 108.

In 2006, F1 ChampBoats returned to the Mississippi for the first time in more than a decade. Champ-Boats are 17 feet long, weigh 1,100 pounds, and are typically powered by a 350 horsepower V-6 EFIMercury outboard. They can reach speeds of 140 mph, and during the turns of a normal fifty-lap event, drivers are subjected to 4 Gs of turning force two hundred times.

In 2006, Spangler Design Team of Minneapolis used art work depicting Kemps Milk Carton Boat Races for the Skipper Pin design. And the Bakken Museum welcomed pirates of all ages to a Pirate's Treasure Hunt. Guests explored a variety of science activities; used maps, compasses and orienteering skills to solve

a beer garden with food, and a Corey Stevens concert on Saturday night. The Marriott Pro Hydrofoil Tour on the mighty Mississippi dazzled spectators and the Aquatennial Arts & Crafts Fair brought shoppers to the

2007 Queen of the Lakes Jessica Gaulke relinquished her crown to serve in the military.

a pirate's mystery; and tried to break the code on the Creative Kidstuff Treasure Chest.

Animaland's Stuff Your Own Collectible Animal event had participants choose from a variety of animals—dogs, cats, elephants, bears, frogs—and then began stuffing it. Personalized birth certificates, cute clothing, accessories and carrying bags were available for the new found friend.

That year Twin Cities Originals (TCO), an organization of independently owned local restaurants, hosted the first ever Taste of TCO event at the Nicollet Island Pavilion. At this culinary gala thirty-two member restaurants served savory samplings.

The Life Time Fitness Triathlon once again offered $500,000, the largest combined cash and prize purse in the history of the sport. Skipper Pins for 2006 still had the skipper wheel and sailboat motif in plastic, but also blinked! Ted Zweig, the Commodore that year, was the first to have served previously as King Boreas of the St. Paul Winter Carnival.

In 2007, Queen of the Lakes Jessica Gaulke, a member of the National Guard, became the first Queen to relinquish her crown to serve in the military. She was stationed in Iraq where she served as a door gunner on a Blackhawk helicopter. The story made national news. ABC News name her Person of the Week. *Glamour* and *People* magazines featured her. Mayor R.T. Rybak declared January 2, 2007 as "Jessica Gaulke Day" in Minneapolis in honor of her military commitment. What an extraordinary individual. She crowned her successor, Jenna Bernhardson, Miss Svenskarnas Dag, at the American Swedish Institute in January of 2007. Jenna reigned over the summer festivities.

The 2007 *Star Tribune* Beach Bash was jammed with fun, what with the Milk Carton Boat Races, the Excel Energy Sand Castle competition, boxing exhibitions, and booths run by the Minneapolis Fire Department, Classic Boats, United Way, Wilderness Inquiry, and other organizations.

Queens of the New Century

Emily Aus

Lisa Carlson

Natalie Neubauer

Megan Harms

Sandra Vucinovich

Marie Hansen

HOPEFUL CANDIDATES

Katie Nelson

Jessica Gaulke

Jenna Bernhardson

Charissa Pederson

Tara Litwinchuk

Alexandra Forster

Alissa Hibst

Amanda Bertrand

Carly Smith

Riley Bruns

The theme for 2008 was Boys of Summer, and representatives from Minnesota Twins teams past and present were the Grand Marshalls at the Torchlight Parade. The Taste of Twin Cities Originals (TCO) returned for a second year. And Bergstrom Jewelers, the official Aquatennial jeweler, sponsored a team of children and their families from the Ronald McDonald House to be participants in the Milk Carton Boat Races.

CenterPoint Energy, sponsors of the parade for the eighth year in a row, marked not only that civic milestone, but also the fact that they had been serving the community for almost 150 years. The parade focused on the history of Minneapolis with the theme "Always There, Through the Generations."

Summer events that year included Labor Neighborhood Block Party, Senior Alumni Karaoke Contest, Star Tribune Beach Bash, Land O'Lakes Sandcastle Competition, CenterPoint Energy Torchlight Parade, Excel Energy RiverBlast, Target Fireworks, and Lifetime Fitness Torchlight Run prior to Torchlight Parade.

A pre-fireworks party called Riverfest was fun, fun, fun! It featured fun, food, and live entertainment. And the sandcastle competition added a category for sculptures of Minneapolis's most recognizable landmarks.

Minneapolis's sister cities sent delegations to enjoy the festivities; it was one of the biggest sister city delegations in history. And the Skipper Pin design returned to a theme from years gone by—a traditional ship's steering wheel.

In 2009 Aquatennial organizers dropped the number ten from their slogan, leaving simply The Best Days of Summer. The Downtown Council organized two

In 2012, Dick Mero appeared in his 71st Aqua parade. It was his 41st year as an Aqua Jester. A quarter-century had gone by since he was inducted into the Clown Hall of Fame set up by Clowns of America International. In 2004 he also served as a Senior Commodore of the Aquatennial. What an amazing legacy!

dozen events and rounded up more than five hundred volunteers to run them. One hundred were needed for Beach Bash alone. That year Eva Brunson Steiner, the first Aquatennial Queen of the Lakes, was the honored Grand Marshall in the Torchlight Parade.

As they have since the Aquatennial's beginnings, civic groups work year after year to keep the Aqua machine running smoothly, for the most part away from

Above and opposite page: Scenes from the *Star Tribune* **Beach Bash**

the public spotlight. Nurses and Red Cross personnel staffed first aid stations, and the Minneapolis Police and Fire departments stand by to deal with emergencies. The Minneapolis Park Board works in tandem with the other groups to unify the programs and services in parades, parks, and other people events, and the Minneapolis Sanitation Department cleans up "the messes." The scope of cooperation from these organizations over

the years deserves many standing ovations.

In 2012, The Minneapolis Aquatennial Association honored the Hennepin History Museum by bestowing upon it the prestigious President's Award for outstanding festival volunteerism. The museum had, for the previous ten years, served as the official repository for the Historic Aquatennial Collection, and had mounted an annual Aquatennial exhibit featuring

The Twin City River Rats

a selection of items from the collection.

New events were added in 2013, focusing on community involvement. Such events included the Roll & Stroll for Mental Health around Lake Calhoun, which benefited Vail Place; a stand-up paddleboard event supporting Avenues for Homeless Youth; and the Midtown Global Music Festival with salsa dancing demos and lessons and salsa samplings.

Meanwhile, at its 18th annual Aquatennial Tennis Classic, many of USTA Northern's best tennis players competed for a $5,000 prize in Men's Singles & Doubles, Women's Singles & Doubles, and Mixed Doubles.

The Twin Cities River Rats again braved the Mississippi River with their tricks, pyramids, and Fly-High jet pack flyer. Midtown Global Market brought dance and live music to celebrate the diverse culture of Minneapolis. A pre-parade kickoff party at Loring Park revved up spectators for the Torchlight Parade with live music, carnival games, and pony rides.

The Aquatennial Goes Green! In 2009, the *Star Tribune* Beach Bash set itself the goal to produce the festival's first-ever "zero waste" event at Lake Calhoun's Thomas Beach, encouraging vendors to use recyclable products and put out recycling containers. In 2013 Metro Transit provided free rides to the CenterPoint Energy Torchlight Parade on busses and light rail. Tap Minneapolis provided water fountains at the Torchlight Parade. Attendees were encouraged to bring their own water bottles and make use of the water stations along the parade route.

Earlier in 2013, as a feature of the Grand Rounds bicycle loop, a kiosk was installed at Theodore Wirth Lake, as a reminder of the Aqua Follies once held nearby. It's hard to imagine today that for twenty-five years, spectacular water shows thrilled audiences from all around the world at Wirth Lake. At the time it was the nation's greatest water extravaganza.

The historic Queen of the Lakes program has developed a new thrust in the 21st century called the Ambassador Scholarship Program. As of 2014, this program will bring Ambassadors to community festivals and will also work toward empowering young women

The *Star Tribune* **Beach Bash**

to enrich communities, organizations, and businesses. The Ambassadors will continue to be active volunteers in a wide variety of programs sponsored by businesses, organizations, and events: the American Cancer Society Daffodil Days, Twin Cities Heart Walk, Alzheimer's Memory Walk, Domestic Violence Awareness Walk, MDA Camp Courage, Ronald McDonald House, Children's Hospital, Third Ward Neighborhoodfest, Pearl Park Picnic in the Park, Salvation Army Bell Ringing, Read-A-Thons, Elementary Classroom Visits, Senior Home Visits, Southwest Super Summer Program, Waite Park Summer Program, Anwatin Middle School Empty Bowls Community Event, and Pageant of Hope.

Queen candidates draw onlookers while relaxing on Lake Minnetonka, ca 1947

We hope you enjoy these little vignettes from behind the tinsel and tulle of the crowns and gowns.

Carol Hall, writing in *Minnesota Good Age* magazine, summed up a young girl's dream: "Aquatennial, especially Aquatennial Queens, figured into my life in the 1950's. Back then many a young girl dreamed of being queen of any event, large or small, but the Aquatennial was the ultimate. To reign over the festival meant pomp and pageantry of the highest order. During the year I devoured newspaper accounts of that year's queen coronation and activities. I was like following a movie star."

&

Coronations have been held in many venues over the years. At one time they were at the Minneapolis Auditorium with audiences of 15,000. The drama and pageantry of these coronations were only one major part of an entire elaborate, celebrity filled extravaganza sponsored by the festival. Many years the coronations were held at Wirth Lake Aqua Follies theatre where, again, it was a part of the overall water spectacular. Other venues have included Parade Stadium, the elegance of the State and Orpheum Theatres, Ted Mann Theatre, Children's Theatre, International Market Square, Radisson Hotel Ballroom, Calhoun Beach Club and at the elegant and acoustical excellence of Orchestra Hall.

&

Many candidates develop a clear idea in the course of the festival of who will be chosen the new Princess or Queen. Often they turn out to be wrong. Sometimes a candidate is stunned when she herself isn't chosen. Most Past Queens agree that with so many outstanding candidates in the running, a different set of judges might easily, and with equal justification, have made different choices.

&

In 1946 *Look* magazine featured a three-page spread on "the land of lakes with sky blue waters." The article referred to Minnesota as the "world's summer playground." The entire article was devoted to the Aqua Queen Candidates, the coronation of the 1947 Queen Ruth Tolman, and her welcome home by her sponsoring city, St. Cloud.

&

When Ken Walstad was executive director he had very tight protocol regarding the placement of the Queen of the Lakes in parades. First would be the local Queen, second would be Miss America if she was attending, and in third parade position would be the

The 1943 Queen was presented with a new bronze and royal purple silk coronation crown.

Queen of the Lakes. If this protocol was not followed, his "Queenie" could not be in the parade.

&

In the late fifties and early sixties, the new Queen of the Lakes was brought to the Leamington Hotel, which was the festival headquarters for years, and ensconced in the magnificent Cinderella Suite. Upon entering, she enjoyed a beautifully appointed sitting room. The oversized bedroom featured a king-sized bed with an elegant gold satin quilted bedspread. Matching gold satin swag curtains framed the head of the bed with beautiful gold satin ballet slippers hanging from gold velvet cording. When the new Queen entered for the first time after coronation, all her clothes had been delivered from the Candidate's floor, and a glittering tiara sat on a satin pillow on the bed. This beautiful suite of rooms would be her home during the ten days of her festival reign.

ॐ

Since 1940, many towns, businesses, and ethnic festivals have chosen queens who went on to become Queen of the Lakes or Aquatennial Princesses. Willmar has had the most with twelve girls followed by Svenskarnas Dag with eleven and Anoka with nine.

ॐ

Difficult as it is to comprehend in the twenty-first century, until the mid 1960's, all Queen Candidates, Princesses, and Aquatennial Queens had their weight, height, age, measurements, and home addresses listed in the newspapers.

ॐ

Queens went through boxes of personalized white stationery embossed with gold letters and a gold crown each year, writing upward of three hundred thank you letters. Beginning in the late 90's, all Aquatennial representatives used a generic thank you card for their hand-written thank you's.

ॐ

Aquatennial's first Queen, Eva Brunson, wore a beautiful, heavy satin formal gown accompanied by an elegant matching satin robe. They were rented from a local costume shop. During the hot summer activities she kept noticing a terrible odor emanating from the ensemble. Being young and embarrassed she did not

GUINDON, 6-27
MINNEAPOLIS TRIBUNE

You know life hasn't been any bed of roses for me, either, being married to an ex-Aquatennial Queen.

dare mention anything about it. Finally, the smell was so overpowering that she told her Commodore, festival founder Win Stephens. He replied he has been wondering for days what the strange smell was. So, Dayton's Oval Room presented her with a stunning organdy dress. Since there was no official crown, white roses and gardenias were made into her halo crown to accentuate the dainty organdy gown.

ॐ

1947 the Mayor of Mexico City presented Queen Ruth Tolman with a complete set of silver jewelry designed and made by the incomparable William Spratling. She still has it and today the pieces are collector's items.

The candidates are escorted by Minneapolis business executives at the Queens Review Luncheon, circa 1967

Judging the Queen Contest

Beth Obermeyer was a guest judge for the 2013 contest. here are a few of her thoughts:

My task was to help a panel of five judges select the next Aquatennial Queen and two Princesses who would travel widely, representing Minneapolis and Minnesota and celebrating community everywhere they went. The judges were eager to find candidates whose personality radiated health, vitality, and wholesomeness. The woman chosen would need to be friendly, photogenic, well groomed, and tastefully attired; and also adept at handling herself with confidence and decorum in unusual circumstances. Educational accomplishments, a spirit of volunteerism, and a history of participation in extracurricular activities would also impress the judges favorably, as would a candidate's manifest desire to make the Aquatennial her top priority for the year.

A few weeks prior to the festival each of five judges received a Judge's Book Manual to study. It contained an 8 X 10 photo of each girl; her information, including her hometown and their annual celebration; her high school and college activities; grade point average (most girls had a GPS of 3.5 or higher); and her opinion on several subjects.

Thus briefed, the judges would begin their work after the girls arrived. The judges mixed in anonymously with the candidates at the Sunday check-in reception, and remained *incognito* during that first day of activities, scattered amid the audience of guests.

On Monday we had our first "official" meetings with the candidates at 7:00 a.m., then later on a boat cruise, at dinner, and at a charity event for Feed My Starving Children. Individual face-to-face judging sessions took place at the Marriott Hotel downtown. We also evaluated the candidates at the IDS Center "Meet the Candidates" program. This was a public event where each young woman wore a theme costume for a short skit she'd designed promoting her hometown festival.

Wednesday night we viewed them in the Torchlight Parade. They were evaluated in formal and informal sessions as well as in formal attire and informal attire; in boating attire and Western attire for a theme party. We looked into their eyes and listened to what came out of their mouths. We watch them interact with one another and with us. I hesitate to admit that the girls were so varied and unique that they almost defied judging.

Yet somehow, by Thursday noon, in all the interviews,

one young woman came across as so sincere and smart, with such a love of people, so talented in so many ways, that she rose above the rest. What we especially noticed was her consistency—no ups and downs. When she answered the final question, drawn from a bowl and written by another contestant, we held our breath. The complicated and sensitive question seemed impossible to answer. She answered, thoughtful, absolutely certain, and unflappable. Now that we had "our Queen," it was a matter of matching two girls to be her Princesses to round out a terrific Royal trio. By Thursday evening we unanimously had the names of the three splendid young women who would be the new Royal Party for 2014, and whose lives would change in a moment at the Friday night coronation.

Within hours the week was over, photos were taken and judges were headed home. We had opened the gates for three girls to a life-changing event. I let them into my heart, but in the end I also had forty-four other new friends and cared very much what happened to them. Each had been chosen by her town or organization, and each had, without exception, represented it with grace and style. Everyone had won where it counted—in her own community, who was so proud of her.

I was amazed at the scale of the planning involved in this operation. For ten years I had planned and executed large scale people events with my event company, Ta Da! Special Events. On one occasion, I organized and led 1,801 tap dancers down Hennepin Avenue to open the arts center. But this week of judging had a variety of special events and many venues—not to men-

tion the organization, housing, transport, and dining of forty-seven young women. Even the judges were treated like royalty all week, ending with the Commodores party Thursday night at Target Field Champions Club. Friday night was a pre-coronation reception and then the Coronation at the Ted Mann Concert Hall.

Was it difficult work knowing I was one of the five whose choices would affect the lives of all these Candidates? Absolutely! And the crown? Its significance in the scheme of things? The tiara is a bit of sparkle the judges added to an incredible woman. From Aquatennial it says "here is one who is dedicated to the importance of celebrating community, one willing to represent us, meet you and enjoy your town and festival and it people. You are part of the Aquatennial family." I am forever honored to have participated in this magical piece of the Aquatennial festivities. I feel part of the festival family.

– Beth Obermeyer

Patty McLane, 1948 Queen, almost wasn't Queen. Upon entering the Aqua Follies arena for the coronation, each candidate was given a bouquet of flowers. Patty thought that her bouquet would look nicer with the dress of Miss Little Falls, the candidate standing next to her. As they were exchanging them, one of the chaperones noticed and quickly stopped the exchange. Patty's bouquet had been specially treated so that when the lights went out, hers would glow, indicating she was the new Queen.

The new official crown worn by Queen Patty McLane (see page 34) was a copy of a crown which won first prize in the exhibition of Arts and Crafts in Florence, Italy, 1906. The design features sterling silver, 24 karat gold-plate, semi-precious stones, red garnets and pearls edged in filigree trim, and genuine ermine.

In 1949, Queen Lee Jaenson wore a king's ransom in jewelry as the "Million Dollar Queen for a Minute." She was photographed in a Crown Jewel necklace assembled from diamonds formerly part of the famous Russian crown jewels and valued at $350,000; a 67½ carat gem-blue pear shaped diamond valued at $100,000; a diamond studded bracelet valued at $50,000. Additionally she wore a dazzling "Spellbound" clip consisting of 782 flawless diamonds that made up a brilliant 212 carats. It required six months' work by three master-craftsmen to match and assemble the piece.

One of the dresses worn by Queen Lee was a walking advertisement for the Aquatennial. The *Minneapolis Star* described it as follows: "Not the dress of seven veils but of seven scarves draped in a spring creation for Queen Lee Jaenson. Activities of the Aquatennial festival are depicted on the 36-inch silk squares. Scarves are available at stores and expected to bring brisk sales." (See photo on page 31.)

1950 Queen, Jean Johnson and BeBe Shopp, 1948 Miss America, were Hopkins High School classmates and had the same church school class.

A wish came true for Helen Jane Stoffer when she filled out an information form for the 1951 Queen of the Lakes candidates. Under "Ambition" she wrote she wanted to be a Registered Nurse. Northwestern Hospital made that dream come true when they presented her with a full three-year scholarship.

On her official trip to France, 1955 Queen Marlene Dolbec received the gift of Pierre, an adorable French poodle. While in Paris she modeled for Christian Dior at his atelier, and later had an audience with the Pope.

1960 Queen Gail Nygaard married 1965 Queen Mary Sue Anderson's brother so they were sisters-in-law.

While on her official trip to Europe, she did a photo shoot for Chanel Coterie. Mme. Gabrielle (Coco) Chanel actually oversaw the shoot while sitting at the top of her famous mirrored staircase. She loved the way Gail looked in her creations. These photos appeared in the Minneapolis Sunday paper.

~

1961 Queen Judy Mellin Colby designed uniforms for the Past Queens Alumni in the early 1960's. Because there were so many various functions to attend, the ladies thought they should present themselves as a group rather than trying to find an individual dress for each occasion. White pique long formal skirts for evening were beautifully enhanced by matching tops with jeweled detachable necklines. For day the top was worn without the jeweled detachable neckline along with a short skirt. Even a maternity top, when needed, completed the elegant look of the ensembles. Of course, long white gloves were de rigueur.

~

In 1962 Queen Pamela Jo Albinson remembers: "It was a chilly, rainy fall day. I had a terrible cold and chills but needed to appear in a small parade in a nearby town. Knowing the convertible top would be up during the parade, I wore long underwear under my sweat suit and put on a heavy coat. As the parade started I fastened the white mink stole over my coat, pinned the tiara into my hair, applied bright lipstick, buttoned up one long white glove for waving out the window from the passenger's seat, clipped on humongous rhinestone earrings and sat

Queens Judy Mellin (Colby, 1961), Eva Brunson (Steiner, 1941), and Joyce Moen (Herrick, 1940), model what they'll be wearing at the Coronation Ball.

with a box of Kleenex on my lap and cough drops in my mouth, gamely smiling through the parade. The glitter of rhinestones, a glimpse of the tiara and royal fur lulled the viewers away from the face of a coughing, wheezing and very sick Queen. But, Aquatennial was represented, and that is what was important.

~

1962 Queen Pamela Jo Albinson wore the same gown that 1960 Queen Gail Nygaard wore at her coronation. Pam, then Miss Anoka, purchased the gown from Gail for $25.00. At the 1961 Queen Coronation Pamela Jo's mother noticed her eight-year-old brother was acting strange and fidgety. When asked why, he said he was worried and wondering what to say to her when she lost.

≈

1963 Queen Connie Haenny wore the same gown that 1961 Queen Judy Mellin had worn at her coronation. Both girls were in Gamma Phi sorority at the University of Minnesota and both were candidates as Miss Flame.

≈

At her Coronation Ball, 1963 Queen Connie Haenny drew the name of the Skipper Pin "Guess the Queen" contest winner. The proud winner of the Pontiac Catalina convertible was Hazel Hawkins Gould, the mother of Connie's high school friend.

≈

From Queen Connie Haenny (1963) regarding her appearance at the Rose Parade: "Everything was so gorgeous. However, behind the flowers and fantasy I was so ill I didn't think I could even make it through the parade. I had chills and a 102 degree fever. We had to be up at 3:00 a.m., dressed formally and in the parade line by 5:00 a.m. for photographs. Because it was chilly we wore long underwear under our formals. I prayed for the parade to end quickly and wondered how I would make the appearance at the football game.

≈

1963 – Barbara Flanagan was Queen Connie's official chaperone on her European trip to England, France, and Germany. Special arrangements were made for her to be able to be in her sister's wedding in Wiesbaden, Germany. While in England, she was the special guest of and modeled for Mary Quant, the designer who gave the world the mini skirt.

≈

In 1969 Queen Janet Johnson traveled 19,000 miles in 19 days, visiting Hawaii, American, Samoa, Australia, Fiji, New Caledonia, New Zealand, and Tahiti representing the festival. It was a whirlwind trip of a lifetime. In Pago Pago, the capital of American Samoa a mini-parade had been arranged in her honor. Waiting for her was a white convertible with a huge sign reading "Talofa Miss Johnson." The streets were lined with great crowds eliciting great enthusiasm. She thought it was amazing that so many were interested in seeing a Queen from Minneapolis, Minnesota. Then she found out they thought she was the daughter of LBJ, the President of the United States.

≈

In the middle of the push for more liberation for women, 1972 Queen Deborah Wolinski recalls being asked to be part of a panel discussion at a University of Minnesota venue only to find herself the subject of derision for perpetuating the stereotype of "being a showpiece wearing a crown." "I felt terribly out of my depth to even defend myself. It was a very difficult few hours. I also remember Ken Walstad, executive director, had an extremely sobering and serious meeting with my two

Volunteering at Feed My Starving Children

A QUEEN CANDIDATE'S PERSPECTIVE

n 2005, Emily Grimshaw represented New Brighton Stockyard Days as a Queen candidate. "The whole week we encountered generous people who wanted to make our candidate week enjoyable. It really wasn't until my week as a candidate that I truly understood the spirit of volunteerism that existed around our state of Minnesota. I realized during my week as a candidate that even if I didn't get crowned, I could still show my love for community by volunteering. The spirit of volunteerism did not escape me as I made sure to stay an active volunteer in my New Brighton community ambassador program as well. Opportunities like the Aquatennial are not only fun, but provide great growth and educational opportunities young inspiring women. The Aquatennial Candidate Foundation was formed, comprised of previous candidates, to continue to volunteer for programs such as Aquatennial that have helped me grow into the woman I am today."

Princesses and me a day after the coronation. He laid out the expectations. Between that and following Maureen Wagner, whom I observed being so utterly poised and at ease, I very nearly opted out due to my fears."

∾

Barbara Peterson, Queen of the Lakes in 1974, became Miss U.S.A. in 1976, and was Grand Marshall in the Torchlight Parade that year. Her husband, Rodney Burwell, was Commodore in 1986. Barbara and Rodney have generously supported a variety of Aquatennial projects over the years, and their contributions were instrumental in securing the purchase of the Dragon Float for the Aquatennial's Fiftieth Anniversary celebration in 1989.

∾

Richard Blackwell, best known for his annual "worst dressed list," was eyeing 1977 Queen Kiki Rosatti's outfit when she was visiting California on an Aqua trip. He looked over at the official necklace studded with the huge aquamarine and the plastic, sprayed gold Aquatennial pin on her dress. With eyes rolling he announced that the necklace was divine but the pin was just too gauche.

∾

The 1982 queen, Lori Werness, met her future husband on an appearance in Two Harbors.

∾

1987 Queen Sandra Polesky was the only Queen to travel to the Wagga Wagga Gumi Festival in Australia. She felt very fortunate because she also went to Japan so had the opportunity to have two international trips representing the festival. "Very eye opening for a small town farm girl!" she stated.

❧

Sara Borg, 1995 Aquatennial Queen from Cokato, greeted her cousin, Juliane Borg from Cokato, when she became 2001 Princess. Sara is married to Craig Holje, Aquatennial Fireworks Director, known as Sparky. Festival people refer to him as "a real blast."

❧

The 2007 Queen, Jessica Gaulke, recalled that the Midosuji Parade down the main street of Osaka, Japan, was the largest parade in which she had ever appeared. It went for blocks and blocks with over a million people applauding the parade units.

QUEEN CANDIDATE COORDINATION

The Queen Candidate program has had an average of forty candidates annually. Early years featured candidates from Minneapolis businesses. In the early 50's more small communities began to participate. Today, ninety percent of the candidates are from communities around the state.

Anne Sumangil, long time director of the candidates program, considers herself fortunate to have had the opportunity to run a program that empowers and elevates young women. Here is her description of the program.

"Planning for the Queen of the Lakes Scholarship program is a year-long process that requires many volunteers and hours and hours of work. The program itself has ranged from five day to nine days, and the candidates are rigorously scheduled most days from 7 a.m. to 10 p.m. This requires coordinating multiple events; scheduling judging sessions including one on one interviews, impromptu and planned public speaking events, panel interviews, public appearances, and networking events; securing sponsorships to offset costs, and managing a hectic travel schedule around the Twin Cities."

Memorable events take place not only on the Candidate bus but also on the Candidate floor of the hotel. For security reasons, the candidates are housed on one floor together and chaperoned by wonderful volunteers during their once-in-a-lifetime experience. Though the program is a very intense, the candidates are assured that this is the one place and the only place during their stay where judges will not be anywhere nearby. The floor has a hospitality room and an off-time meeting place to hang out, receive deliveries of flowers, cards, and gifts, and imbibe a myriad of refreshments.

To assist in whatever is needed during that time, a small but devoted group of special volunteers—the Men in Black—are on hand. The group was started by the sons of chaperones who acted as gofers and security guards for the young women during the week and especially at parade time.

CHAPERONING THE QUEEN OF THE LAKES CANDIDATES

At the conclusion of the festival each July, organizers begin planning immediately for the following year's events. So, too, do the chaperones of the 35 to 50 Queen Candidates who will be arriving from all over the state. They design master schedules for the young womens' week, incorporating activities from morning to late evening, which are then coordinated with the Royal party's schedules. Potential sponsors are contacted, especially for private bus transportation and food/restaurant service, prizes, printing, and other incidentals. Suddenly plans are almost in place and it's festival time!

On check-in day chaperones greet the young women, who are eagerly anticipating their jam-packed week. The chaperons have already studied each candidate's bio, but now they begin to truly get to know these young women, who all have different personal needs and personal agendas. They're a study in human nature.

It soon becomes evident that some candidates truly want to win, some don't think they have a chance, and some don't even think about winning. Some have no interest in becoming a Princess: they only want to be considered for Queen. Some tell the judges not to consider them at all, because they would be unable to devote a year to the festival for one reason or another. Some feel that the honor of being their local community's queen is enough.

Some young ladies just want to enjoy the week and give no thought of the outcome. Others arrive ready, willing and able to serve, but have a change of heart in the course of the week, doubting whether they could fulfill the expectations of the royal role for an entire year.

The week is all about the candidates, but the chaperones typically have as much fun as the girls. The candidates are cared for, listened to, encouraged, given a shoulder to cry on, given respect, dignity, while being lovingly chaperoned at all times. Always on deck, the chaperones are available to handle a myriad of unforeseen circumstances. Individual judging days present a cacophony of emotions, but the chaperones know and understand how to handle these situations. At all their appearances, the candidates are introduced or must introduce themselves and their communities. This is frequently followed by short speeches which can prove unnerving. But, the young women can always rely on the chaperones for a "thumbs up!"

Each year the Candidate bus is their limousine, emblazoned with Queen Candidates banners on both sides. Some years they even have a double decker bus. One of the favorite bus drivers was "Mike, the bus driver," ala Mike Rossini. With daring do, for many years, he proudly escorted the girls around the city, keeping them on their tight schedule at all times. He heard their stories, laughed their laughs, sang their songs, and was an important component in making their week the best ever. "Bus bonding" is an important ingredient for "getting to know you," and because the girls have to sing for their supper, so to speak, original songs are devised, improvised, and rehearsed enroute to their appearances. Mike knew and could sing them all.

Two special events stand out for chaperones Bill and Duffy Sauer. One of the most anticipated scheduled events for many years was the candidate trip to the Minneapolis Veterans Home. Lunch was served, and then the young ladies mingled and conversed with many of the veterans. At times they were fortunate enough to encounter veterans from their communities, so they could share a bit of local color. Many Polaroid photographs were taken, and, years later, chaperones found, upon return visits, the photos were still lovingly placed in the rooms. As the candidates boarded the bus to return to their hotel, many had tears streaming down their faces.

Another memorable event occurred in 1989. Barbara Peterson Burwell, 1974 Queen of the Lakes, and her husband, Rodney Burwell, 1986 Commodore, hosted an elegant dinner party at their magnificent home on Lake Minnetonka. Tents were set up for dining. All the candidates were to arrive wearing their white coronation formals. It was pouring rain, unfortunately. When the candidate bus arrived, it got stuck at the bottom of the long drive to the house which is situated on a hill. The girls courageously trekked up to the house and were escorted to the second floor in preparation

Barbara Peterson Burwell and her husband Rodney in 1986

for their individual introductions. Each one graciously proceeded down the elegant curved staircase. Once all introductions were made to the dinner guests, the Sibley marching band entered the foyer and loudly enlivened the festivities. The rain has caused havoc, even on the dampened tent floors where dinner was served. Hence, about eleven girls had their white coronation gowns wet and dirty from the escapade. But, Barbara was on top of the situation. The soiled dresses were handed to her, and in exchange, she graciously handed back to each of the "rained-on eleven" an extra-large black plastic garbage bag to wear on her journey home. Then she made arrangements with a local dry cleaning establishment to have the gowns ready within 24 hours for the girls' next event. All's well that ends well and this event certainly did. The jokes and laughter regarding the latest in garbage bag fashions did not abate all week.

The chaperones agree that these shared experiences are always the best of times and saying good-bye to these wonderful young women the morning after coronation is heart wrenching. But the incomparable memories and friendships live on!

Organization and Responsibilities

In the course of three quarters of a century, many millions of people have enjoyed the parades, performances, contests, and other events sponsored by the Minneapolis Aquatennial. Behind the scenes, a far smaller group of volunteers and community leaders has worked, year after year, to insure that the festival remains vibrant. Although the Aquatenial's organizational structure has changed from time to time, it can be conveniently divided into three functional groups: business, Ambassador, and festival.

Until recently, the business side of the Aquatennial was managed by the Minneapolis Aquatennial Association, headed by the Aquatennial President and the Aquatennial Board of Directors. This association focused on policy, strategic planning, and finances. The Aquatennial policies were periodically reviewed by the Board of Directors, and Board of Director Strategic Planning Committees addressed the Aquatennial's future and took actions to ensure that both festival events and community outreach conformed to the festival's mission. The board also maintained an annual budget to support the festival and its Ambassadorial functions, keeping a close eye on fundraising and operational expenses.

A Vice President offered assistance to the President, assuming responsibilities that varied but were usually directed towards membership, public relations, marketing, Skipper Pins, and concessions. This position was discontinued after 1986.

The Ambassadorial arm of the Aquatennial,

headed by the Commodore and the Queen of the Lakes, was responsible for representing the Aquatennial and the City of Minneapolis at events and community festivals throughout the State of Minnesota and selected national and international festivals. The Ambassador group also included the two Princesses, the President, the General Festival Chair and the Vice Commodores. It was the responsibility of the Commodore to escort the Queen of the Lakes, and of the President and General Festival Chair to escort the Princesses. Appearance scheduling required that the Vice Commodores would also act as Ambassadors and escorts for the Queen of the Lakes and Princesses at various events and community festivals.

Additional Ambassador groups included the senior and junior contingents: Senior Commodore, Vice Commodore, Queen, and Princess; Junior Commodore, Queen, two Vice Commodores and two Princesses. The Junior Ambassador group was discontinued in 2001.

The operations of the festival itself were the responsibility of the General Festival Chair and the Vice Commodores. Typically, the Aquatennial festival was divided into five divisions: Parades, Hospitality, Sports & Lakes, Special Events, and Metro and Youth. As festival programming varied, other divisions were temporarily added: Mississippi River Showcase, Show & Awards, Arts and Entertainment, Ambassador, Powerboat Classic, etc. The Metro and Youth Division became the Community Division in 1987.

It was the responsibility of this group to plan and execute the entire festival under the direction of the

Above: In 2001, the Senior Ambassadors were (left to right) Clyde Durrand, Betty Larson, Eunice Roberts, and John Montour.

Below: One of the last sets of Junior Royal Ambassadors.

General Festival Chair. Each festival division likely included several related events. Groups of events within a division were the responsibility of a coordinator, and each individual event the responsibility of a chair. The aspects of each event requiring attention included content, logistics, marketing, budgeting, and execution.

In addition to planning and executing the Aquatennial festival, the General Festival Chair and Vice Commodores made occasional Ambassador appearances, escorting the Queen of the Lakes and Princesses.

The positions of General Festival Chair and Vice Commodores were replaced in 1995 by the position of Captain. The festival portion of the Minneapolis Aquatennial was taken over by the Minneapolis Downtown Council in 2002. At that time there was a clean break between the festival side of the Minneapolis Aquatennial and the Ambassador group. The Downtown Council produced all of the festival events with its own volunteer base and the Aquatennial Ambassador Organization (AAO) became responsible for the Ambassadors and their appearances during the Aquatennial festival and at other community festivals and events throughout the year. The newly formed Captain position became part of the Ambassador group.

There are four Ambassador alumni groups that are part of the Aquatennial Ambassador Organization: Admirals (past Commodores and Presidents), Past Queens, Past Princesses, and Commanders (past Vice Presidents, General Festival Chairs, Vice Commodores, and Captains). Each of these alumni groups sponsors a social event during the festival which includes hosting the Queen of the Lakes Candidates.

Aquatennial Volunteers

The Minneapolis Aquatennial is a volunteer organization. Without a doubt, Aquatennial excels in having "blue ribbon" volunteers; volunteers who are part of an enormous, logistical, well-oiled, and experienced machine that has been in operation for seventy-five years. Despite overwhelming challenges and impossible odds, they continue to contribute vitality and a "can do" attitude by donating their time, talents, and dedication in planning, executing, driving, serving, helping, and working in any and all capacities to carry the festival message. Aquatennial's award winning volunteers can be counted on to bring new ideas and energy to the long held traditions.

Aquatennial, over the years, has had a very small budget. The only paid staff has been the Executive Director, and three assistants. In the late 80s the yearly cost of running the festival approached $300,000. Corporate and individual memberships plus the Skipper Pin sales bring in revenue. Otherwise, the events are free. The three thousand dedicated volunteers from all strata of the festival pay all their own expenses. Uniforms, luncheons, dinners, coronations, extensive travel, and a multitude of other expenses come out of personal pockets, not Aquatennial funds.

The only recipients of all expenses paid by the Aquatennial Association are the Queen and the two Princesses. Frequently the Commodore and President of any given year pay for additional expenses, which can be considerable. Every year the Aquatennial gives out the cherished Kenneth Walstad Award to one of the most devoted festival volunteers.

Aquatennial Admirals Club

The Aquatennial Admirals Club is the alumni group of Presidents and Commodores who provided overall leadership to the Minneapolis Aquatennial.

During the Aquatennial's formative years, past Presidents and Commodores met informally. Then in the early 1950s, the Admirals Club was formed by a group of past Presidents and Commodores to provide an organized structure to help continue the traditions of the Aquatennial and support the festival. Throughout the decades, many Admirals have served on the association board, as committee chairs, and have provided significant financial support to the Aquatennial.

The Admirals select a member of the club as Grand Admiral to preside over club activities for a two-year term. The Grand Admiral then recruits a club member to serve as Fleet Admiral. The Fleet Admiral assists in planning activities for the club and succeeds the Grand Admiral when their term expires. During Ken Walstad's tenure as Executive Director of Aquatennial, he arranged well attended quarterly dinner meetings of the Admirals Club at the Radisson South.

Soon after the club was organized, members decided that the Admirals should have unique uniform coats to wear during Aquatennial and club functions, replacing their formal white coat. Selected for members, the new coat was a very distinctive light blue jacket, with the appropriate accouterments. A pocket patch was designed for Admirals to wear on a dark-colored blazer on less formal occasions.

At the end of their year of service to the Aquatennial, the outgoing President and Commodore are invited to attend the Admirals Club meeting held annually in the fall at the Minikahda Club.

In the early years, the initiation of members was elaborate and creative. Prospective members were taken to the outdoor pool after dinner, instructed to remove their shoes and coats, and to put on lifejackets in preparation for being thrown in the pool (this was in October). After an appropriate amount of taunting and preparation, club members would decide that they would not subject the prospective members to the splash party. A variation of this was to advise the aspiring members well in advance of the meeting to be prepared to "walk the plank" at the annual meeting and to plunge into the pool. Again, after some haggling between the members and the prospective members, it was decided that dunking would not be required. Then, upon returning to the Minikahda Club dining room, members would "roast" the aspiring members and also ask many challenging questions about their "qualifications and suitability" for membership. After the members were satisfied as to their qualifications, a vote was taken to admit them to the club.

Each year brought creative and humorous initiation activities. One of the best initiations was the year that an outgoing President and Commodore were provided with sandwich boards that promoted banks that competed with the bank where they were employed. The prospective members were then directed to parade through the lobby of the Radisson South wearing their sandwich boards and distribute advertising material for the competing bank.

The Admirals organized and managed a separate private foundation that was funded by members and outside donors. For many years, the foundation provided the annual scholarships to the outgoing Aquatennial Queen of the Lakes and Princesses as they completed their respective reigns.

Aqua Seniors Rock

In 1979 the Aquatennial Senior Alumni Association, Inc. (MASAA) incorporated as a fully volunteer non-profit association of approximately sixty seniors age 55 and over to support the Minneapolis Aquatennial celebration. That same year the group was officially inducted into the historic Aquatennial Royalty. The first Senior Royalty sponsored by the Government Center and the telephone company were Senior Queen Margaret Grimmes and Senior Commodore Stanley Antolak. Seniors developed such events as a 500 Card Tournament, a River Walk, and a coronation luncheon. Bingo games were sponsored for the Minneapolis Veteran's Home. Aquatennial also invited them to attend specified Aquatennial events, especially the parades, wearing their Navy type uniforms of navy jackets and white slacks

In 1984, Marge Mapson, Elsie McDonald and Floyd Bosshardt started the Aquatennial Senior Singers, a chorus group of six who performed at city nursing homes. The Singers, now thirty-five members strong, are a significant mainstay of the Senior Alumni events and continue to perform year round at dozens of senior residences and other venues in the Twin Cities area. They bring a refreshing mix of religious, patriotic, humorous, and popular songs, ending with their theme song," Hey, Look Me Over!"

In 1998 additional events were added to the Senior's repertoire. Queen Aggie Swanson initiated and chaired the Formal Dance. In 1999 she added the Senior Bowling Tournament as well as Senior Queens' and Princess' wardrobes.

A major Senior Alumni distinction was the selling of the Skipper Pins. For years, Doris Battenberg and Eunice Andren each sold many hundred of pins. Some years they individually sold more than a thousand pins. In 1997 Doris sold 1,175 pins.

Since 1997 all candidates for the Senior Alumni Royalty positions have been invited to become members of the Senior Alumni Association and become involved in all the events, activities, and fellowship of the group.

In 2001, when the Aquatennial festival events were transferred to the Minneapolis Downtown Council, the Senior Alumni group was split off on its own. Coordination of the senior events is now under control of the Senior group. The seniors are dedicated to continuing their Aquatennial legacy and contributing to the well being of city seniors.

CONGRATULATIONS, MINNEAPOLIS AQUATENNIAL,
FOR 75 YEARS OF CIVIC PAGEANTRY, ENTERTAINMENT,
COMMUNITY INVOLVEMENT,
AND TRADITION!

Acknowledgments

Thank you, or "my sincere gratitude," become inadequate phrases when it comes to the passion of Aquatennial lovers who have brought this historic book to life. It has been a unique and collaborative effort. It is regrettable that many of the people who have contributed to the festival's success over the years cannot be named, but they are included in hearts of Aquatennial lovers and enormously appreciated.

Such acknowledgement extends to the Minneapolis Downtown Council, festival officials, Aquatennial Association Directors, Admirals, Captains, Commanders, members and sponsors, staff and vendors, whose loyalty, imagination, hard work, and commitment of countless hours have made the Minneapolis Aquatennial "America's Greatest Summer Festival" year after year.

I would like to mention by name a few of the individuals who made important contributions to this book. I have known many of them for years. Some agreed to formal interviews, others wrote short essays that I have incorporated into the text, not all of them explicitly acknowledged. Others contributed in some other way by sharing unusual artifacts or sharing memories on the phone: Karen Althen (Parrington), Jaclyn Auger, James Bacigalupo, Sarah Bell, Charlie Boone, BA Breese, Sharon Carlson, Rick Collins, Sharol Enger, Juliann Enroth, Donna Erickson, Jennifer Erickson (Evers), Jim Erickson, Alexandra Forster (Lindstrom), Jessica Gaulke (Rainey), Emily Grimshaw, Connie Haenny (Baker), Ken and Eileen Hafften, Doug and Ann Hair, Bruce Humphrys, Gregg Johnson, Tom LaSalle, Judy Mellin (Colby), Neil Messick, Jr., Beth Obermeyer, Jim Patterson, Robert Perkins, Barbara Peterson (Burwell), Nancy Piazza, Suzanne Polkey (Berg), Dave Recker, Katie Fornasiere, Duffy and Bill Sauer, Brenda Schuler (Pehrson), Denny Schulstad, Fred Smith, Anne Sumangil, Sandra Vucinovich, Sonja Weiler, John Wetzel, Bernie White, and Leah Wong.

On a more personal level, my appreciation goes to Jack Kabrud, Curator of the Hennepin History Museum and Susan Larson-Fleming, Museum Archivist. You two amaze me! They became festival supporters when, in 2002, it was brought to their attention that the festival's archival materials were in a storage center with no place to call home. These two historic minded experts were the initiators and solid supporters of having the Museum become the official repository for the historic Aquatennial collection. Their commitment to its preservation during the last ten years has been overwhelming. And Jack's creativity in designing outstanding Aqua exhibits during festival week has filled unique niche as an added event. Because of him, an archive that might appear to someone as just a frayed souvenir booklet, or just an ancient uniform, or just a crown, suddenly appears in an awe inspiring exhibit vignette. Throughout the years, special segments of the festival have been exhibited and honored such as Senior Royalty, Aqua Follies, Junior Royalty, Aqua Jesters, crowns and gowns, parades and floats. Susan and Jack have been uncompromising in their expertise with the Aquatennial archival preservation. Such preservation has been significant in having incredible historical materials for this book. Susan's expertise as an editor added significantly to the book's journey towards proud publication.

John Toren, Nodin Press editor and designer *par excellence*, has probably learned more about Aquatennial than he ever imagined possible. Processing and designing all the various pieces of information into the resultant gem this book is, has been his focus for months. He had a vision as to how 75 years of "bits and pieces" should cohesively come together. Hence, this remarkable product. It has been my utmost pleasure to work with John, an incredibly creative, sensitive, almost Renaissance man with a terrific sense of humor. He kept me on track. Thank you, John, for the privilege of working with you. You brought such care and creative understanding to our Aqua history.

What an incredible honor to have Barbara Flanagan, admired for years by so many, especially her *Star Tribune* readers, take the time to write the foreword for the book. Barbara, your years of Aquatennial involvement, including chaperoning many Queens on their foreign trips, brings wonderful perspective to these treasured memories.

But, most important of all, huge hugs go to Norton Stillman for believing in the festival and caring enough to make the possibility of this book a reality. Expressions of appreciation are impossible to convey to you, Norton, our "Aquatennial Angel." How you have honored Minneapolis and Minnesota history with your belief in the merits of producing this book. The richness of your contributions on every level has made it possible to bring alive amazing memories for ever so many, forever. You are a treasure!

About the Author

Pam Albinson, Miss Anoka, became Minneapolis Aquatennial Queen of the Lakes in 1962. During her official year she traveled 150,000 miles and made more than 600 appearances. Her foreign trip coordinated by Senator Hubert Humphrey and accompanied by Anoka newspaper editor/owner Arch Pease and his wife, Amy, took them for three weeks to South America, where they were the honored guests at the Carnival in Rio. The trio also made scheduled visits as sister city and civic/business representatives promoting tourism and trade for the Aqua City. These appearances garnered elaborate publicity for Minneapolis and Minnesota. Cities visited were Rio, Brasilia, Montevideo, Buenos Aires, Sao Paulo and Lima, Peru. For the past ten years she has compiled the Aquatennial history for the Hennepin History Museum, the official archival repository for the Aquatennial collection. Her passion for history and the essential role it plays in preserving and expanding our cultural heritage underlies every aspect of this collection of festival remembrances.

AQUATENNIAL AMBASSADORS ALUMNI

2014
Queen Riley Bruns – Annandale
Commodore Dave Hutton
Princess Alison Gunter – Clara City
Princess Jeni Haler – Waconia
Captain Karen George
Captain Gary Schaak
Senior Queen Kathy Reimer
Senior Commodore Frank Gurney
Senior Princess Jann Smeltzer
Senior Vice Commodore Bernie Flegelman

2013
Queen Carly Smith – Red Wing
Commodore David Recker
General Festival Chair Lindsey Peterson
Co-President Jim Patterson
Co-President Tom LaSalle
Princess Anna Surprenant – Sleepy Eye
Princess Leah Kruc – Fridley
Captain Sonja Weiler
Captain Sharolyn Carlson
Senior Queen Judy Harding
Senior Commodore Bruce L. Humphrys
Senior Princess Roxanne Denysiuk
Senior Vice Commodore Terry Lee Hoppenrath

2012
Queen Amanda Bertrand – Montevideo
Commodore Tom LaSalle
President Ted Zwieg
Princess Cayla Yund – Cambridge
Princess Stephani Reding – Maple Grove
Captain Jennifer Brentano
Captain Brent LaSalle
Senior Queen Jan Christianson
Senior Commodore Peter King
Senior Princess Cheri Blood
Senior Vice Commodore Lou Michaels

2011
Queen Alissa Hibst – Svenskarnas Dag
Commodore Bill Hogan
President Ted Zwieg
Princess Alyssa Carlson – Fridley
Princess Gina Collings – Hutchinson
Captain Jennifer Brentano
Captain Brent LaSalle
Senior Queen Cindy Shanley
Senior Commodore Pat Bohmer
Senior Princess Ellen Johnson
Senior Vice Commodore Jim Graham

2010
Queen Alexandra Forster – Delano
Commodore Jim Patterson
President Bill Rissmann
Princess Abbrielle Massee – Hopkins
Princess Angela Kron – Svenskarnas Dag
Captain Jim Domeier
Captain Daryl Wahl
Senior Queen Pam Askeland
Senior Commodore Dave Ulvin
Senior Princess Shirlee L. Callender
Senior Vice Commodore Pete Koegel

2009
Queen Tara Litwinchuk – Maple Grove
Commodore Thomas LaSalle
President Bill Rissmann
Princess Jaclyn Auger – Hutchinson
Princess Emily McConkey – Cokato
Captain Natalka Hertaus
Captain Rob Mauzy
Senior Queen Lyn Kay Henderson
Senior Commodore David Gasparrini
Senior Princess Gwendolyn Jefferson
Senior Vice Commodore Donald Lucas

2008
Queen Charissa Pederson – Monticello
Commodore Mary Niemeyer
President Bob Alfton
Princess Jenna Forstner – Gibbon
Princess Tzvetelina Pramatarov – Anoka
Captain Rob Mauzy
Captain Lindsey Peterson
Senior Queen Ann Hair
Senior Commodore Douglas Anderson
Senior Princess Judy Holmquist
Senior Vice Commodore Pat Bohmer

2007
Queen Jessica Gaulke – Robbinsdale (July-Jan)
Queen Jenna Bernhardson – Svenskarnas Dag (Jan-July)
Commodore John Hines
President Joe Johnston
Princess Jenna Bernhardson – Svenskarnas Dag (July-Jan)
Princess Lindsay Saunders – Willmar
Princess Nichelle Hackert – Anoka (Jan-July)
Captain Bob Clark
Captain Matt Mcdonough
Senior Queen Betty Hein
Senior Commodore Doug Hair
Senior Princess Janice Wilbur
Senior Vice Commodore Joe Jenson

2006
Queen Katie Nelson – Paynesville
Commodore Ted Zweig
President Jim Erickson
Princess Jill Starke – Annandale
Princess Jintana Nelson – Blaine
Captain Tim Rose
Captain Nick Koch

Senior Queen Jerilynn Bergeson
Senior Commodore David S. Bennett
Senior Princess Louise Leininger
Senior Vice Commodore Art Stumne

2005
Queen Marie Hansen – New Brighton
Commodore Mark Stenglein
President Jackie Cherryhomes
Vice President John Brant
Princess Susan King – Maple Grove
Princess Amanda Spaeth – Sleepy Eye
Captain Glen Sorenson
Captain Eric Steege
Senior Queen Judith Swanholm
Senior Commodore Robert Clark
Senior Princess Marjorie Douville
Senior Vice Commodore Dean Leininger

2004
Queen Sandra Vucinovich – Lakeville
Commodore Jim Erickson
President Jackie Cherryhomes
Princess Sarah Strom – Maple Grove
Princess Courtney TerWisscha – Clara City
Captain Skip Nelson
Captain Mark Stenglein
Senior Queen Vernie Bjorklund
Senior Commodore Dick Mero

2003
Queen Megan Harms – Lake City
Commodore John Brant
President LisaRenee Gratz
Princess Kelly Brose – Howard Lake
Princess Berit Ahlgren – Svenskarnas Dag
Captain Skip Nelson
Captain Ollie Kaldahl
Senior Queen Lorraine Beversdorf
Senior Commodore Lyle Bay

2002
Queen Natalie Neubauer – Hutchinson
Commodore Joe Johnston
President LisaRenee Gratz

Princess Heather Mumaugh
Princess Anna Millerbernd – Waverly
Captain Tamara Fleischhaker
Captain John Montour
Senior Queen Phyllis Chickett
Senior Princess Liz Johnson

2001
Queen Lisa Carlson – Willmar
Commodore Nancy Lindahl
President Wendell Willis
Princess Juliane Borg – Cokato
Princess Anne Sumangil – Crystal
Captain Louis Ryg
Senior Queen Eunice Roberts
Senior Commodore John Montour
Senior Princess Betty Larson
Senior Vice Commodore Clyde Durand

2000
Queen Emily Aus – Granite Falls
Commodore Jerry Noyce
President Donna Erickson
Princess Dayna Cervin – Litchfield
Princess Summer Nelson – Cambridge
Captain Joe Johnston
Captain Vollie Sanders Sr.
Senior Queen Jeanne Joseph
Senior Commodore John Luchessi
Senior Princess Helen Kokes
Senior Vice Commodore Richard Kloos

1999
Queen Kelly Gahlon – Willmar
Commodore Stu Voigt
Chairman Mike Grimes
President Denny Schulstad
Princess Jennifer Sedey – Delano
Princess Laura Spaeth – Sleepy Eye
Captain Lezlee Vrieze-Cole
Captain Carolyn Cleveland
Senior Queen Jeanne Mason
Senior Commodore Vollie Sanders Sr.
Senior Princess Edie Sultze
Senior Vice Commodore Don Erickson

1998
Queen Carrie Nevitt – Glenwood
Commodore Cornell Moore
President Mike Grimes
Princess Katie Hendrickson – Svenskarnas Dag
Princess Brooke Cebulla – Buffalo
Captain John Brant
Senior Queen Cynthia Desonpere
Senior Commodore Jim Lanenberg
Senior Princess Dorothy Litvany
Senior Vice Commodore Jim Mason

1997
Queen Christine Scherping – Melrose
Commodore Denny Schulstad
President Bill Rissmann
Princess Shawna Bodenhamer – Cokato
Princess Sara LaDue – Anoka
Captain Robin Plaisted
Captain Jack Mertes
Senior Queen Marian Huard
Senior Commodore Mike Mickelson
Senior Princess Fran Larson
Senior Vice Commodore Donavan Hinrichs

1996
Queen Bethany Hibbard – East Bethel
Commodore Charlie Boone
President Bill Rissmann
Princess Dawn Welch – Hopkins
Princess Shannon Zeig – Sleepy Eye
Captain Steve Anderson
Captain Clinton Collins Jr.
Senior Queen Carol Hill
Senior Commodore Paul Bengston
Senior Princess Jane Myre
Senior Vice Commodore Bob Hamlett

1995
Queen Sara Borg – Cokato
Commodore William (Bill) J. Popp
President Bob Jaskowiak
Princess Joy McDonell – Willmar
Princess Jennifer Peterson – Annandale
Captain Ken Hafften

Senior Queen Agnes Swanson
Senior Commodore Jim Battenberg
Senior Princess Luella Reininger
Senior Vice Commodore George Sellner

1994
Queen Robyn Johnson – Crystal
Commodore Louis DeMars
President James (Jamie) R. Lowe III
General Festival Chair Jody Lingofelt
Princess Jennifer Dock – Anoka
Princess Karrn Gustafson – Cambridge
Senior Queen Jeanne Jeffords
Senior Commodore Joe Cohen
Senior Princess Elizabeth Lee
Senior Vice Commodore Ludvig Pafko

1993
Queen Kacie Cassidy – Robbinsdale
Commodore Dave Cleveland
President Dennis McGrath
General Festival Chair Bob Eastman
Princess Karen Althen – Richfield
Princess Renee Anderson – Svenskarnas Dag
Senior Queen Mary Yoshida
Senior Commodore Don Cregan
Senior Princess Marion Swanson
Senior Vice Commodore Stanley Crist

1992
Queen Brenda Flury – Rockford
Commodore Dean Terry
President Rick Collins
General Festival Chair Dave Anton
Princess Jacqueline Hakes – Crosby-Ironton
Princess Natalka Kramarczuk – Northeast Minneapolis
Senior Queen Lenora Finley
Senior Commodore Ralph Thacher
Senior Princess Vernice Peterson
Senior Vice Commodore Clarence Daugaard

1991
Queen Lisa Gratz – Crosby-Ironton
Commodore James Hearon III
President Robert Perkins

General Festival Chair Ken Hafften
Princess Kristi Bennecke – Anoka
Princess Sarah Kodet – Svenskarnas Dag
Senior Queen Eunice Andren
Senior Commodore Ken Covington
Senior Princess Marion Koch
Senior Vice Commodore Joseph Davis

1990
Queen Jennifer Munson – Fridley
Commodore George Carisch
President Robert Perkins
General Festival Chair Jack Breese
Princess Lisa Gohman – Maple Lake
Princess Amy Machacek – Defeat of Jesse James
Senior Queen Patricia Marble
Senior Commodore Stanley Eddy Jr.
Senior Princess Bev Scherfenberg
Senior Vice Commodore Elbert Collin

1989
Queen Barbara Stockdill – Golden Valley
Commodore William S. Reiling
President Joseph Foss
General Festival Chair Bill Rissman
Princess Lori Kuefner – Miss Dassel
Princess Diane Vagle – Hutchinson
Senior Queen Evelyn Young
Senior Commodore Tillman Stevens
Senior Princess Florence Stull
Senior Vice Commodore Howard Helland

1988
Queen Jennifer Tolrud – Richfield
Commodore Lee R. Anderson
President John E. Derus
General Festival Chair Rick Collins
Princess Kerri Heckenlaible – East Bethel
Princess Anne Swanson – Svenskarnas Dag
Senior Queen Lorraine Dysart
Senior Commodore Charles Saarion
Senior Princess Renza Anderson
Senior Vice Commodore Orville Prestholdt

1987
Queen Sandra Polesky – Sleepy Eye
Commodore George Murnane, CLU
President Lee Johnson
General Festival Chair Mike Geiser
Princess Ann Minks – Princeton
Princess Jody Peterson – Ham Lake
Senior Queen Loretta Salie
Senior Commodore Vern Tatton
Senior Commodore Walter Sochacki
Senior Princess Elsie McDonald
Senior Vice Commodore Les Scherfenberg

1986
Queen Julie Melin – Sons of Norway
Commodore Rod Burwell
President Frank Anton
General Festival Chair Bill Pearson
Princess Maria Borash – Cambridge
Princess Ann Rime – Willmar
Senior Queen Irene Novak
Senior Commodore Floyd Bosshardt
Senior Princess Mable Swanson
Senior Vice Commodore Gerald Cook

1985
Queen Lori Grote – Red Wing
Commodore Daniel F. May
President Stanley Tabor
General Festival Chair John T. Wetzel, Ph.D.
Princess Janet Schotzko – Sleepy Eye
Princess Brenda Schuler – Granite Falls
Senior Queen Marge Mapson
Senior Commodore Richard Schneider
Senior Princess Josephine Anderson
Senior Vice Commodore Lester Dundas

1984
Queen Jody Hempel – Annandale
Commodore Carl G. Pohlman
President Raymond J. Dittrich
General Festival Chair Luanna Hacker
Princess Polly Benson – Anoka
Princess Colleen Mahoney – Heartland
Senior Queen Fay Cassidy
Senior Commodore Leonard Thompson

1983
Queen Amy Mertes – Miss Fire Fighter
Commodore Fred Bassinger
President Gerald Pettersen
General Festival Chair Cynthia Williams
Chandler
Princess Rhonda Anderson – Svenskarnas Dag
Princess Belinda Phelps – Two Harbors
Senior Queen Eleanor Mueller
Senior Commodore John Wallace

1982
Queen Lorrie Werness –
Svenskarnas Dag
Commodore Woodrow P. Langhaug
President Edward Fish
General Festival Chair John Hohl
Princess Kathy Fuller – Windom
Princess Diane Rivard – Fridley
Senior Queen Ella Friedlund
Senior Commodore Marvin Warholm
Senior Vice Commodore Harold Geiger

1981
Queen Cathy Linsmier – Hopkins
Commodore Harold W. Greenwood, Jr.
President Douglas M. Head
General Festival Chair Chris Christofilis
Princess Lisa Beytien – Hutchinson
Princess Leanne Evans – Litchfield
Senior Queen Mary Shonka
Senior Commodore Bing Crosby

1980
Queen Mary Jo Dillenburg – Willmar
Commodore Darrell Runke
President Fredrick Dresser
General Festival Chair David Hutchins
Princess Kristin Knudsen – Sons of Norway
Princess Jayne Siewert – St. Cloud State Home-
coming Queen
Senior Queen Edna Memtom
Senior Commodore Hagbarth Bue

1979
Queen Becky Rear – Montevideo
Commodore Gil Braun
President Fredrick Dresser
General Festival Chair John Hanlon
Princess Linda Johnson – Columbia Heights
Princess Robin Rhode – Sauk Rapids
Senior Queen Margaret Grimes
Senior Commodore Stanley Antolak

1978
Queen Sharolyn Frampton – Anoka
Commodore Harry Atwood
President Frank Pazlar
General Festival Chair William McKinney
Princess Mary Jane Houts –
Svenskarnas Dag
Princess Janelle Urdahl – Litchfield

1977
Queen Katherine (Kiki) Rosatti – St. Cloud
State University
Commodore Edward Fish
President Clair W. Kjome
General Festival Chair Edward A. Cunnington
Princess Wendy Ostlund – Hopkins
Princess Shelley Stenberg – Buffalo

1976
Queen Catherine Steinert – Robbinsdale
Commodore Robert L. Johnson
President John F. Stone
General Festival Chair George Murnane, CLU
Princess Sheila Andrade – Ministerial Alliance
Princess Pam Jasper – Spring Lake Park
Princess Susan Monahan – LeSueur
Princess Debra Kay Schmidt – Miss Flame

1975
Queen Anita Abraham – East Minneapolis
Commodore Richard "Dick" Enroth
President Richard "Dick" I. Halvorsen
General Festival Chair Bert L. Ehrman, Jr.
Princess Pam Erickson – Glenwood
Princess Jeanne Schulze – LeSueur

1974
Queen Barbara Peterson –
Svenskarnas Dag
Commodore G. Robert Werness
President Jack W. Nicols
General Festival Chair Lee Johnson
Princess Vicki Johnson – Robbinsdale
Princess Sandra Lies – Annandale

1973
Queen Patricia Kelzer – Shakopee
Commodore Lloyd "Bud" Swanson
President Jerome S. Yugend
General Festival Chair Al Schutta
Princess Deborah Hanson – Willmar
Princess Candy Johnson –
Svenskarnas Dag

1972
Queen Deborah Wolinski – North Minneapolis
Commodore Eugene W. Woolley
President Vern M. Gust
General Festival Chair Robert Antila
Princess Karen Cook – Miss Flame
Princess Kathy Massich-Micheletti – Hibbing

1971
Queen Maureen Wagner – Hopkins
Commodore Richard H. Massopust
President James B. Delano
General Festival Chair Robert Morshare
Princess Jarolyn Warner – Willmar
Princess Barbara Williams – Bemidji

1970
Queen Annette St. Dennis – Anoka
Commodore Reuben L. Anderson
President Milton S. Boyce
General Festival Chair Lee Lemieux
Princess Carole Van Valkenburg – Golden Valley
Princess Susan Theis – Gopher State Timing
Association

1969
Queen Janet Johnson – Winona
Commodore Russell T. Lund
President Donald W. Peterson
General Festival Chair C. J. McConville
Princess Heidi Gustafson – Miss Flame
Princess Terri Polish – Bemidji

1968
Queen Karen Hegener – U. of M. Engineers Day
Commodore Milton S. Boyce
President Everett M. Taft
General Festival Chair Richard B. Brown
Princess Bonnie Lietzau – Hutchinson
Princess Maria Swinsisky – East Minneapolis

1967
Queen Karen Erlandson – Cokato
Commodore Carl A. Hustad
President James J. Finnegan
General Festival Chair Allen Benzick
Princess Rita Couet – Granite Falls
Princess Nancy Purcell – Anoka

1966
Queen Linda Kleinert – East Minneapolis
Commodore Carl N. Platou
President Albert H. Heimbach
General Festival Chair Vern Gust
Princess Ann Mueller – Golden Valley
Princess Cyndy Odland – Granite Falls

1965
Queen Mary Sue Anderson – Willmar
Commodore Alan H. Moore
President Sherman K. Headley
General Festival Chair Edwin S. Dygert
Princess Jean DeVilliers – Golden Valley
Princess Mimi (Gretchen) Krieger – Southdale
Ford

1964
Queen Mary Margaret Schultz – St. Cloud
Commodore O.D. Gay
President William G. Preston

General Festival Chair Robert F. Granquist
Princess Margaret Dredge – U. of M.
Engineers Day
Princess Suzanne Sheets – Hopkins

1963
Queen Connie Haenny – Miss Flame
Commodore T. Floyd Cullen
President Robert Witte
General Festival Chair Paul Mans
Princess Patricia Lund – St. Cloud
Princess Pam Taylor – Donaldsons

1962
Queen Pamela Jo Albinson – Anoka
Commodore Robert Gisselbeck
President Lawrence "Duke" Johnson
Chief of Staff Rodney S. Wallace
Princess Darlene Anderson – St. Louis Park
Princess Judy Halverson – Willmar

1961
Queen Judy Mellin – Miss Flame
Commodore Onan A. Thompson
President Mark T. Spinner
Princess Judith Nelson – Svenskarnas Dag
Princess Marlene Rignell – East Minneapolis

1960
Queen Gail Nygaard Anderson – Willmar
Commodore Philip C. Smaby
President Lyman D. Walters
Princess Marsha Gaviser – U. of M.
Engineers Day
Princess Sharon Miller

1959
Queen Sharon Bigalke – St. Louis Park
Commodore Randy Merriman
President Reynold C. Malmquist
Princess Barbara Erickson – Prudential
Princess Mary Olson – Willmar

1958
Queen Pat Wilson – Granite Falls

Commodore Ellsworth L. Johnson
President John M. Diracles, Sr.
Princess Sheila Boyle – Local 1145
Princess Barbara Theilen – North Minneapolis

1957
Queen Mary Erickson – Prudential
Commodore M. Wayne Field
President F. W. Mitchell
Princess Joan Freeberg – Golden Valley
Princess Jackie Hanson – U. of M. Engineers Day

1956
Queen Judy Penny – Uptown
Commodore Wells Wright
President Otto A. Silha
Princess Barbara Tennis – Edina
Princess Diane Clarely – Wayzata

1955
Queen Marlene Dolbec – Local 1145 Honeywell
Commodore Karl F. Diessner
President Robert W. Blackmur
Princess Margaret Ellefson – Glenwood
Princess Nancy Jensen – Fergus Falls

1954
Queen Betty Trones – Richfield
Commodore J. Leonard Larson
President Harold J. Anderson
Princess Mary Forester – Mankato
Princess Gloria Shopek – Minneapolis Aqua
Jesters

1953
Queen Joanne Melberg – Robbinsdale
Commodore Neil R. Messick, Jr.
President William A. Benson
Princess Pat Biethen – Rochester
Princess Dawn Joyce – Uptown Club of
Minneapolis

1952
Queen Betty Barnhart – Hopkins
Commodore Emmett L. Duemke

President Russell C. Duncan
Princess JoAnne Claesgens – St. Cloud
Princess Annella Marthaler – Sauk Centre

1951
Queen Helen Stoffer – Golden Valley
Commodore Evald C. Bank
President Theodore B. Knudson

1950
Queen Jean Johnson – The Dayton Company
Commodore Lee Potter, Jr.
President David Silverman

1949
Queen Lee Jaenson – St. Cloud
Commodore Carl T. Bremicker
President W. N. Dickson

1948
Queen Patty McLane – The Dayton Company

Commodore Bert Baston
President George M. Jensen

1947
Queen Ruth Tolman – St. Cloud
Commodore Donald R. McReavy
President Joyce A. Swan
1946
Queen Marilyn Lindstrom – Army
Commodore Gerald L. Moore
President Frank J. Collins

1945
Queen Nancy Thom – Women's Army Corps
Commodore Tom Hastings
President Edward Schlampp, Sr.

1944
Queen Patty Carlson – Coast Guard
Commodore Tom Hastings
President Neil R. Messick, Sr.

1943
Queen Barbara Matson – Navy
Commodore Neil R. Messick, Sr.
President Herbert W. Ward

1942
Queen Vivian Hofstad – Sears Roebuck
Commodore Tom Hastings
President Neil R. Messick, Sr.

1941
Queen Eva Brunson –
Northwestern Bell
Commodore Winfield R. Stephens
President Tom Hastings

1940
Queen Joyce Moen – Fergus Falls
Commodore Winfield R. Stephens
President Tom Hastings

JUNIOR AMBASSADORS

(Junior Queen, Commodore, Princesses, Vice Commodores)

1949   Carolyn Rose Herrmann

1950   Dawn Haehn

1951   Gail Ann Blankenhorn

1952   Lynn Miller

1953   Diane Matelsky

1954   Nancy Jo Piazza

1955   Suzanne Polky, Gregory Johnson

1956   Catherine Bergstrom, Robert Dolan

1957   Barbara Leighton., Everett Beadle

1958   Kathleen Nulvehill, Bobby Norwick

1959   Rhonda Malison, Larry Schroeder

960   Jane Hoffman, John Jarnig

1961   Missing

1962   Linda Claypathch, Carl Weis

1963   Monijo Buzzelli, Bruce Meyer

1964   Susan Wilharm, Bruce Varmer

1965   Linda Johnson, Michael Albrecht

1966   Linda Johnson, Timothy Boys

1967   Robin Beebe, Paul Belvedere

1968   Julie Bjoin, Allan Currie

1969   Marci Gittleman, Christopher Polzin, Renee Collins, Coleen McCombs, Terry Burgoyne, Scott Meckle

1970   Jill Gerling, Derek Dragotis

1971   Julie Farmer, Derek Dragotis

1972   Jodie Hagstrom, Chip Liabratten

1973   Linda Lelija, John Larue, Angela Nelson, Donna Jo Smuda, Derek Oldfatheer, Randy Gorsegner

1974   Tanja Kozicky, Daniel Flemming, Jennifer Stans, Maureen Neighbor, Tom Deretich, Christopher McGraw

1975   Jennifer Bush, Ray Kieffer, Andrea Larson, Meg McDonough, Joseph Fleming, Erik Redepennin

1976   Jennifer Link, David Abele, Kristine Zechmeistser, Lisa Smith, Christian Lebens, Terry Fleming

1977   Rosanne Garvin, Dain Martinez, Anastasia Larson, AnnMarie Donahue, Timothy Star, Mark Thomas

1978   Jessica Minion, Tyrone Workman, Michelle Castillo, Erin Neighbors, John Zajac, Tim Link

1979   Tiffany Wells, Steven Noon, Jr., Tracey Peterson, Marni Thompson, Dean Erickson, Greg Gagnon

1980   Sherry Engel, Robert Baarson, Coleen Cava, Krista Johnson, Todd Monroe, Michael Bjorn

1981   Tamera Nelson, Bryce Darnell, Catina Krull, Annemarie Techam, Shawn Johnson, Ross Sadoff

1982   Marni Moore, Jon Meldo, Renee Mageshwari, Melissa Ahman, Mark Oreschnick, Gavin Rydell

1983   Tania Wolverton, Keith Lowinske, Desiree Wren, Laura Mae Rivers, Travis Littlefield, Stuart Mitchell

1984   Jennifer Olson, Jacob Blumer, Angela Hering, Stephanie Kukatchka, Michael Johnson, Peter Moore

1985   Angela Forte, Joseph McIntosh, Maryann Nalec, Lori Delaitsch, Jeremy Sayther, Sean Erickson

1986   Alison Johnson, Todd Perien, Alisha Howard, Erin Ingvalson, Tony Scavo, Jonathan Wright

1987   Jessica Bari, Jeremy Schad, Michelle Durand, Sarah Morris, Brad Nixa, Brandon Nelson

1988   Carolyn Ly, Tony Gable, Gerilyn Mortenson, Sara Roberts, David Roberts, Stefan Faust

1989   Sarah Graham, Justin Hendirckson, Carissa Getty, Heather Rice, Anthony Plaisted, Dominic Fleetham

1990   Rose Amber Sutton, Matthew Meunier, Angela Forsgren, Emily Windsor, Robert Gardner, Kevin Taafee

1991   Megan Bailey, Eric Sodergren, Ali Ingvalson, Jennifer Castellano, Tim Gregerson Jr, David Serber

1992   Crystal Meagher-Hiltunen, Paul Peterson, Whitney Erickson, Angela Slavik, Tony Haugen, Danny Orr

1993   Bethany Doran, Matthew Dittes, Lynn Moore, Rachel Serber, David Hedges, Ronald Wachter

1994   Heather Eastwold, Brett Strickland, Mackenzie Will, Elizabeth Cerepak, Joshua Finsrud, Andrew McLean

1995   Megan Ranta, Brady Ervin, Brittany Thelemann, Tandehl Collentine, Buddy Castellano, Max Headline

1996   Chelsie Carpenter, Alex Haspert, Amanda Kuchelmeister, Kelsey Hanzely, Neil Boehlke, Corey Swamsno

1997   Ali Dahl, Alex Zonn, Alyssa Miskowic, Katie Hanson, Maxwell Fadipe, Robert Durant

1998   Brianne Blum LeMire, Michael Goeldi, Sarah Damerow, Danielle Klein, Adam Godes, Justin Carlson

1999   Emily Manske, Taylor Isle, Amy Neguse, Katelyn Seawell, Sam Stark, Justin Heidelberg

2000   Laura Zaworski, Joe Laue, Robin Conama, Brittany Kapala, Kyle Jevnager, Teddy Leighton

2001   Lauren Myers, Mikey Killingham, Whitney Buchelt, Amanda Apple, Brandon Marine, David Palmer